THE WAR ON
WARRIORS

ALSO BY PETE HEGSETH

Battle for the American Mind:
Uprooting a Century of Miseducation

Modern Warriors:
Real Stories from Real Heroes

American Crusade:
Our Fight to Stay Free

In the Arena: Good Citizens, a Great Republic,
and How One Speech Can Reinvigorate America

THE WAR ON
WARRIORS

BEHIND THE BETRAYAL OF
THE MEN WHO KEEP US FREE

PETE HEGSETH

HarperCollins books may be purchased for educational, business, or sales promotional use. For information, please email the Special Markets Department at SPsales@ harpercollins.com.

Fox News Books imprint and logo are trademarks of Fox News Network, LLC

FIRST EDITION

Designed by Michele Cameron

Library of Congress Cataloging-in-Publication Data has been applied for.

ISBN 978-0-06-338942-7

24 25 26 27 28 LBC 5 4 3 2 1

For the American fighting man—past, present, and future

Proclaim this among the nations:
Consecrate for war;
stir up the mighty men.
Let all the men of war draw near;
let them come up.
Beat your plowshares into swords,
and your pruning hooks into spears;
let the weak say, "I am a warrior."

—JOEL 3: 9–10 (ESV)

Contents

Introduction

THEN THEY CAME FOR THE CAMOUFLAGED CLASS

I joined the Army in 2001 because I wanted to serve my country. Extremists attacked us on 9/11, and we went to war. I became an infantry officer in 2003. I guarded terrorists at Guantanamo Bay in 2004. I led men in combat in Iraq in 2005. I pulled bodies out of burning vehicles in Afghanistan in 2012. I held a riot shield outside the White House in 2020.

And, in 2021, I was deemed an "extremist" by that very same Army.

Yes, you read that right.

Twenty years... and the military I loved, I fought for, I revered... spit me out. While writing this book, I separated from an Army that didn't want me anymore. The feeling was mutual—I didn't want *this* Army anymore either.

I could have stayed in, which would have required renewing my top secret security clearance—and an extensive background check. I've done it many times before. No sweat. I have nothing to hide. But, to put it plainly, I don't trust this government, this commander in chief, or this Pentagon. That's not to say the situation is permanent—hence this book—but my trust, for this Army, is irrevocably broken.

Over the last two decades, I lived the story of this book. Saw it and fought it—firsthand. And will share some of those stories with you.

I'm a civilian now, but my fight continues. Starting with this book.

The War on Warriors is written for my sons—and yours. Future soldiers, maybe. They will either save, or surrender, our Republic.

* * *

Given what I wrote above, you'll be surprised by the next sentence. Now is not the time to retreat from our military. If we secede from our military branches—and service writ large—then we're handing the keys of our Republic over to people who *loathe* the sort of men vital to defending us.

Our "elites" are like the feckless drug-addled businessmen at Nakatomi Plaza, looking down on Bruce Willis's John McClane in *Die Hard*. But there will come a day when they realize they need John McClane—that in fact their ability to live in peace and prosperity has always depended on guys like him being honorable, powerful, and deadly.

The military has long been a place for turning mere boys into fighting men not just by teaching them honor and sacrifice but by channeling daring, building strength, and accumulating skills. The so-called elites directing the military today aren't just lowering standards and focusing on the wrong enemy; they are overtly working to rid the military of this specific (essential) type of young patriot. They believe power is bad, merit is unfair, ideology is more important than industriousness, white people are yesterday, and *safety!* is better than risk-taking.

However, our enemies still understand that a soldier needs to be powerful, skilled, and courageous. Sometime soon, a real conflict will break out, and red-blooded American men will have to save their elite candy-asses. You may not want your sons or grandsons to enlist right now, but teach them to be powerful, skillful, and brave; when war comes—and it will, abroad or at home—that's what will win it for us. The only way we can fight back against the Left's antiwarrior radicalism is to recover a true vision of the value of strong men, the importance of normality, and a true sense of honor.

It would be easy to lose faith. But looking at the sweep of American history shows this isn't the first time that the military has been under-mined by feckless civilian leaders and foolish brass. Generals have always chosen certain groups to discriminate against. Over the years, the iden-tity of the disfavored class of soldiers has shifted from one group to an-other. Positive change happens when those disfavored soldiers commit to serving even in an imperfect force.

No matter how bad things are for the American military—and things are really bad—I believe I will not be the last Hegseth to wear the uniform I love.

This book is a clarion call to charge ahead with everything we have into the breach. Retreating now means we will definitely lose. Charging ahead means we have a fighting chance.

The military is where our country needs—desperately—patriotic, faith-filled, and brave young Americans to step up and take the long view. At a basic level, do we really want only the woke "diverse" recruits that the Biden administration is curating to be the ones with the guns and the guidons?

But more than that, we want those diverse recruits—pumped full of vaccines and even more poisonous ideologies—to be sharing a basic train-ing bunk with sane Americans. If elite universities are where underprivi-leged kids learn how to hobnob with the elites, then the military should be where potential Antifa members learn what it really means to use force for just and honorable reasons. The American military is one of the great deradicalization machines for aimless young men—but only if it's working correctly.

The United States military was designed to act as the immune system of America's sovereignty. The reflexive snap to repel harm. The tireless sentry for threat. The promise of consequence against foes of freedom. Always has been, always should be. Yet America, and her military, are going quietly into the night. Powerful leftists have leveraged their disdain for America to systematically confuse, neuter, and weaken the greatest fighting force for good this world has ever seen. It happened, and is still happening, rapidly.

Don't just take my word for it, here are the folks who wrote the book on it. Each year, the Heritage Foundation publishes its *Index of U.S. Military Strength*. Think of it as a 650-page report card for every branch of the U.S. military. Its 2024 report is blunt, "as currently postured, the U.S. military is at significant risk of not being able to defend America's vital national interests." For the second year in a row, our military is rated as "weak" relative to the force needed to defend national interests.

Weak . . . two years in a row. The authors of this exhaustive report are patriots. Most are former military. They love our troops. And they are brutally honest. Things must change, and quickly—for the sake of our country and our warfighters.

* * *

The failure to acknowledge the sacrifice and goodness of the American fighting man is nothing new. As soldiers often say, "Shit rolls downhill"—and has since gunpowder was invented. The failures of civilian leadership often fall on the shoulders of our nation's warfighters—not only minimizing their valor but marginalizing their sacrifice in pursuit of postwar political priorities. The Afghanistan retreat debacle is the most obvious contemporary example, but this trade-off is not unique to my generation.

The veterans of Bataan and the Death March of 1942 returned home after years of torture and abuse in Japanese POW camps, some already bitter that their own government left them in the Philippines without any resources or hope of rescue. In the 1950s, the United States government concluded a treaty with Japan that included a secret clause prohibiting the Death March survivors from suing any of the Japanese companies that used them as slave labor during the war. In return, the Japanese turned over all their chemical and bacteriological weapons research, some of which was based on experiments with the very same Allied POWs who were now unable to ever receive compensation for abuse they suffered.

That breach of trust destroyed those men's faith. One Bataan survivor said, "I love my country. It's the government I can't stand."

The troop surge in Iraq put Sunni tribes and American infantry shoulder to shoulder to fight Al Qaeda and Iranian-backed militias; just one year before, Sunnis and Americans were shooting at each other. It was a temporary marriage of mutual interest and a moment of confusion for many ordinary American soldiers. Yet amid even the most confusing and unbearable moments on the battlefield, we at least believed our military leadership had the best interest of our men and their mission at the center of their intent, and in their hearts.

Today, this is clearly not the case.

When confronted with the warped, woke, and caustic policies of our current military—which this book will outline—political leaders and general officers (aka politicians in camo) espouse clever obfuscations about the purpose of our military ("Diversity Is Our Biggest Strength" being the absolutely dumbest of them all). They seem to think that somehow "Be All That You Can Be"—the long-touted and recently revived Army recruiting slogan—is more about personal growth, levels of diversity, and self-expression than deterring and, if need be, defeating the enemies of America. We've become a "You Be You" military.

Civilian leadership and military discipline are foundational to who we are. But what we really seek, what we need—and what we crave—is military leadership that fiercely preserves the core purpose of the military *and*... political leaders who don't treat the 101st Airborne like Harvard University. Our troops are fighters, not gender studies freshmen. They could have enrolled in college if they wanted more indoctrination, but instead they serve. This is more than simply a misunderstanding, or a difference of priorities—it's a fundamentally different view of the purpose of warriors.

I reserve my greatest scorn not for politicians because, well, they're politicians. Radical leftist leaders will push radical leftist prerogatives, consequences be damned. The real blame falls on the military itself. The question of this book is not: How did the military go woke? The real question is: *How did the military allow itself to go woke?*

You see, this time is different. We all know America is experiencing a massive and dangerous cultural and political change. In the past few decades—after nearly one hundred years of spade work—radical leftists have captured nearly every American institution: universities, corporations, media, Hollywood, social media, K–12 public schools, the federal bureaucracy, and even most mainline churches. Their goal was stated very clearly by Barack Obama: fundamentally transform America. You don't "fundamentally transform" something or someone you love; you transform something you disdain. As Mark Levin recently documented, the Democrat Party really does hate America. Our Constitution, our flag, our faith, and our creeds.

Now, they have come for our camouflaged class. The exact same thing is happening to the United States military, only at a *much* faster pace. For decades, the military remained mostly insulated from cultural capture—courageous men took their oath to the Constitution seriously and didn't allow fundamentally unserious and unconstitutional ideas to infiltrate the ranks. Then, at first slowly but then quickly, that dam broke. New military leaders, at best, uncritically parroted the bad ideas of civilian leadership; at worst, they sold out our military.

It's one thing when a corporation or university goes "woke." It's an entirely different thing for the United States military to go woke. It's *fucking* scary, and I've had a front-row seat—along with a generation of warriors, most of whom are now getting out *and* not encouraging their kids to join. Where does that end? How does it end? Not well, that's for sure—unless we do something about it.

* * *

The winnowing fork of the military has always existed, serving to separate the wheat from the chaff—those able, ready, and willing must earn their spot, their rank, their reputation. For most of American history, this culling was based on a soldier's eagerness and willingness to demonstrate technical proficiency, obey lawful orders, and lead or follow with courage. (The label "soldier" will often be used in the book, and—unless specifically referred to as an "Army soldier"—represents all service members. My apologies in advance to all the Sailors, Marines, and Airmen who will feign outrage!)

What we have today, and what we cannot accept, is a military *intentionally* enacting policies that repel, repulse, and remove eager and willing troops. Our military cannot survive a long-term infection of radical left-wing social justice policies designed to isolate, resegregate, and stigmatize certain troops based on a specific racial, gender, or political philosophy.

Our military cannot survive the intentional cratering of "good order and discipline" in the name of "equity." Standards ignored, at every level and in every realm.

The military was the first large, national institution to be successfully racially integrated (despite the interference of racist presidents like Woodrow Wilson). Yet today's troops are being harassed by obligatory training—and eventually "standards"—grounded in Critical Race Theory, radical sex theories, gender policies, and "domestic extremism" that are designed to neuter our fighting forces. In the name of going forward, we are going backward, destroying our military from within. And, yes, it's intentional. Just ask all the perfectly healthy, young troops the Pentagon kicked out because they wouldn't take an experimental vaccine with unknown side effects. (And now the Pentagon wants them back—because recruitment is plummeting. Most have given Uncle Sam an unvaccinated middle finger.) The Left must control everything—and, today, they are obsessed with controlling, and neutering, our military.

The military cannot be organized like a Harvard fraternity, catering to ever more obscure constituencies. Our key constituency is normal men, looking to be heroes and not victims. Ordinary men, willing to be extraordinary—or die trying; for God, country, and their brothers. We aren't a collection of aggrieved tribes. Equality is our bedrock, lethality our trademark. There is no black and white in our ranks. We are all green. Our strength is *not* in our diversity, but in our unity and in our love for each other, our families, and, most of all, our nation. We have standards, and we enforce them—with consequences. This is a truth I have lived firsthand.

It is with this understanding that I share the warning of this book and stand with all veterans to serve and protect the Constitution of the United States of America—against all enemies, foreign and domestic.

I fought to defend freedom, but it's become impossible to defend *this*.

If our military, and our Republic, ever truly usurped my constitutional oath and bowed fully to the tyranny of the Left, then—to use a historical example—I would leave the British Army of 1775. I would stand and fight, and advise my kids to find a bridge in Lexington and Concord to stand their ground with me. What does that look like in a world of F-35s and hypersonic missiles? I don't know. This is why *The War on Warriors* (the working title of this book was "Battle for the American Military") is so closely tied to my previous book, *Battle for the American Mind*—because if we don't stay free, then we're just another country with a flag. I won't fight for just any flag, and I hope my kids would not either.

* * *

This book is personal to me because I let all this happen. My generation fought foreign wars—overemphasizing their importance—while leftists crept into our domestic culture and institutions, and are now doing the same to our combat units.

This humble soldier—who loves God, his family, and his country—won't now sit on the sidelines and simply bemoan the state of our country and military. We are awake to their woke; and our battle begins anew, here at home. Make no mistake about it: the Left wants to destroy the one institution standing between them and total control—the United States military.

In *The War on Warriors*, I describe how we got here, what the threat is, the Left's mode of attack, and how we can take back the high ground to save our military. Like the issue of education, if we fail, we fail all future generations of America. It's one thing to lose our classroom; it's another to lose the ability to execute close-air support or deter communist China. If we lose our military, the world's last best hope is toast. And then freedom is toast—because that military, eventually, will be turned on us.

You don't need any more explanations of why our enemies hate us. We can all turn on MSNBC if we want to hear that. We need more reminders that America is good, young American men can be brave, and that there's a damn good reason why people flee their shithole countries to reach our shores. Those seeking America know what the Left wants us to forget: that our country is not a systemically racist colonizer state, but a systemically free constitutional state.

If we can keep it.

If we want to live free, we'd better be willing to die trying.

The American fighting man gives our country the prime of their lives, slamming headlong into combat, without any concern for what tomorrow will bring. Unlike our enemies, we don't fight because we hate what's in front of us, we fight because we love what's behind us. We fight so our kids may inherit that which can only be purchased with blood: our God-given constitutional freedoms and rights.

John Stuart Mill once said, "War is an ugly thing, but not the ugliest of things: the decayed and degraded state of moral and patriotic feeling which thinks that nothing is worth a war, is much worse."

The minute we believe our freedoms "inevitable and immutable," we cease to live in history, and have soured the soldier's sacrifice. Our freedoms—purchased on the battlefield—are "worthy of war."

As odd as this sounds, I don't want you to "enjoy" reading this book. There are some fights that we can win, and there are other fights that we cannot afford to lose.

The War on Warriors is that fight. We cannot lose.

THE WAR ON
WARRIORS

Chapter 1

THE WAR WE MISSED

Confidence in the American military has reached the lowest level in two decades. Military recruiting numbers have plummeted, across all services—and continue to sink. Army bases I served at—and millions of warriors trained at and deployed from—have been given benign new names like "Fort Liberty." Our generals are hunting for racists in our ranks that *they know* do not exist. Meanwhile, affirmative action promotions have skyrocketed, with "firsts" being the most important factor in filling new commanders. *We will not stop until trans-lesbian black females run everything!* The Afghanistan failure reverberated worse than anyone expected, with not a single leader responsible held accountable. Headlines like "China Wins in Central America" are commonplace, a pardon was granted to an American soldier who walked off his base into enemy hands, and the secretary of defense decided to be AWOL for a week, and not tell anyone.

This is just the beginning, but for me—and my generation—it's personal. How in the world did we get here?

* * *

After fighting against an external radical Islamist ideology for twenty years, America's veterans (generally speaking) were exhausted—and our ranks thinned and confused—by fighting a war on two fronts. On the one side, many of us fought in a foreign war, making temporary allegiance with neoconservatives who, in the moment, defended a war we believed in. But, on the home front, the Left never stopped. Then-senator Obama's defeat of Senator John McCain in 2008 left many of us feeling deflated—the wars were doomed, and a young, untested leftist was in charge. That election didn't cause us to give up, as much as it created paralysis and confusion in our ranks. We were on the outside, not sure what our country just voted for. Like a disgruntled spouse, we hoped a cooling-off period would help. Some of us even supported Obama's "surge" in Afghanistan—putting politics aside for the warriors still fighting. I even visited the Obama White House in 2009 to offer my support for the Afghanistan surge. And later volunteered to serve in Afghanistan for a year. I wanted to defeat the enemy for Team America. *How quaint of me.*

Having seen *real* enemies on the battlefield, we naively hoped it would be apparent to reasonable people that America—despite our mistakes—was the best thing going. If you've seen Baghdad, even Baltimore looks like Beverly Hills.

We could not have been more wrong.

While the post-9/11 generation of patriots spent two decades fighting enemies abroad, we allowed America's domestic enemies at home to gobble up cultural, political, and spiritual territory. Overextended, our rear guard was exposed—and the enemy pounced. (Republicans and conservatives at home did a really shitty job holding down the home front, to say the least.)

What we eventually discovered is that just like an enemy at war, the radical Left never stops moving and planning. They do not respect cease-fires, do not abide by the rules of warfare, and do not respect anything except total defeat of their enemy—and then total control. They consistently attack without regard for reciprocity or fairness. They are willing to fight by any means necessary, which includes destroying the very Constitution that cloaks their treason. The radical Left never takes a day off and uses every avenue—political, cultural, and educational—to push its agenda.

Antifa, BLM, now Hamas supporters and other progressive storm troopers have done their best to create little Samarras (the Iraqi town I was deployed in) in the center of cities like Portland, Chicago, Minneapolis, Seattle, New York, and San Francisco. Places where police must respect the indigenous populations of street addicts and operate under a bizarre set of rules of engagement that effectively cede the territory (neighborhood) to the enemy (criminals). People who offer no resistance to their political ideology are steamrolled—as the fundamental transformation is afoot. The modern progressive Left shows no shame when they trash our laws, nor do they pretend to uphold their own constitutional oaths of office.

They are the law, the police, the prosecutor, the judge, the jury, and executioner. And it happened fast, while America's best warriors were wearing camouflage and fighting halfway across the world. The Left didn't fight the wars. They stayed home and wrecked our house. America-wreckers, all of them. These domestic extremists are the real American "Jody"—ask a veteran; they'll tell you.

The Left's audacity and hubris allow them to ignore the laws they don't like and then prosecute the people they don't like. Legislation doesn't matter, and former presidents are their targets. They do so while we sleep, while soldiers return to the safety of our civilian lifestyles, and while we seek to earn a living and raise our children under the liberties guaranteed by the very Constitution we fought for. All of this is allowed by the creation of a new (un)holy writ, by abrogation of the Constitution and through a social justice filter that our progressive institutions have taught for years to a generation of kids—who are now incapable of seeing Truth, or loving their country.

* * *

Real Truth doesn't change. Not "your truth" or mine, but *the* Truth. Inside a Republic, the first-line countermeasure to revisionist meddling is understanding and defending the American institutions that were designed to be our True North. The best defense against the lies of the enemy is a confidence in the goodness of our history, our constitutional system, and our freedoms.

In my aforementioned book, *Battle for the American Mind*, we peeled back the onion on why, and how, the American Left took control of K–12 education to capture, and remake, America's families, culture, and eventually politics. This was not a project the imperialistic Left conceived in my lifetime, but one that existed well before my parents were born. Even my grandparents. Like the Islamic terrorists that we fought in Iraq and Afghanistan, the project is not of their generation. It moves through generations of zealots and revolutionaries. This has been an objective of the American Left since the turn of the twentieth century. It is ongoing. It never stops. It's unrelenting.

Battle laid out how recapturing American classrooms for Western-Christian values will be difficult, if not impossible. We are eighty years behind the Left, and they are dug in. We are still losing ground. The book defined the problem, described how we got here, paid homage to the timeless educational truths we abandoned, and outlined how we can get them back. In short, we sounded the alarm about a century-long problem, death by a thousand cuts—all happening under our noses until we couldn't ignore it anymore.

This book is different.

This book comes at a moment—and I write this without hyperbole—that we should be in panic mode. Almost desperate. Willing to do anything necessary to defeat the "fundamental transformation" of the American military and end the war on our warriors. In *Battle for the American Mind*, based on the longevity and sheer power of the Left's educational takeover, we argued for an "educational insurgency"—a tactical retreat from the educational system to regroup, save our/your kids, and build new, faith-filled schools.

The War on Warriors calls for the exact opposite. In this book, there is no time—or room—for an insurgency. The Left captured the military quickly, and we must reclaim it at a faster pace. We must wage a frontal assault. A swift counterattack, in broad daylight. If we wait for nightfall, they will regroup. If we retreat from the system to rebuild, it's gone. And building another American military is not an option. We have only one Pentagon. One secretary of defense. One Army. If we lose it—we are toast.

The transformation of the American military, as you will learn, has been rapid—but not nearly as complete as the Left's capture of the classroom. If we are to recapture the military—and we must—it must happen quickly, and soon. Otherwise, we will lose. The current woke victory is broad, but it is not deep. The shoehorning of Diversity, Equity, and Inclusion (DEI), Critical Race Theory (CRT), feminism, genderism, safetyism, climate worship, manufactured "violent extremism," straight-up weirdo shit, and a grab bag of social justice causes that infect today's fighting force have nothing to do with making our military more capable. They are anathema to everything the American military stands for; a natural antibody is poised to kick in, if we fight to unleash it. It will take stone-cold leadership, unbending courage, and an unyielding fidelity to the Constitution. If we give the social justice wokesters time to dig in—to entrench—then the American military will cease to exist as a real fighting force—except against our own people.

* * *

As stated earlier, civilian control of the military is one of our core constitutional principles, with the president serving as the commander in chief. While Congress is tasked with funding the military—and overseeing the use of that money—only the president can ask Congress to approve a declaration of war. And Congress formally authorizes war—but it rarely works this way, especially in the modern era. This arrangement is supposed to be a central feature of our Constitution. However, in the wrong hands, it is problematic—because these checks and balances are too often ignored. With the command and control exerted by the president's executive branch, the military can be used to transform the behaviors of the citizen-soldiers in ways that the civilian population—namely voters and their elected representatives in Congress—would never allow. This can be used for good (like racial integration), but also for ill. The recognition of this enormous power demands perpetual vigilance be applied to how the military can be used extraconstitutionally by a rogue or radical executive branch. As I said earlier, the military doesn't just go woke; it must allow itself to go woke.

Respect for civilian leaders doesn't equate to total obedience to them.

Just because someone serves in the military does not mean they have no constitutional rights. To state it bluntly, the realities of warfare—especially for those of us who have seen it firsthand—supersede the necessity to obey illegal commands that manifest in weakening the force and getting troops killed. This understanding, which requires fidelity to the Constitution, military values, and actual readiness, is what should keep our soldiers from the manipulations of leaders who want to use the military for their own social experiments. Every soldier swears an oath to the Constitution, nothing else, and should never bend a knee to a politician, a party, or a philosophy—let alone one that is an enemy to that very same Constitution. Again, politicians with radical social philosophies—from Woodrow Wilson to Barack Obama—come and go; the real story is how an institution founded on fidelity to the Constitution has allowed itself to be captured by anti-American, anticonstitutional Marxist philosophies.

While waging war is mostly left to the military, there are numerous instances of direct presidential management of military affairs—in times of both war and peace. Only once, in the early days of the Republic, did a president command troops in the field. George Washington put his uniform back on and led thirteen thousand federal troops to put down the Whiskey Rebellion. He later regretted the action, believing it could set a dangerous precedent.

From that moment on, the actions of commanders in chief have always had political consequences, many of which end up being unpopular. It took Abraham Lincoln multiple tries to land on a winning general. Harry Truman's sacking of General Douglas MacArthur during the Korean War sent shock waves through the military and political ranks for decades. Our defeat in Vietnam put an end to Lyndon B. Johnson's political career and left our military rudderless. *It turns out LBJ wasn't good at picking specific military targets.* Jimmy Carter followed suit, culminating in the infamous failed Iranian hostage rescue mission known as "Desert One."

Despite good, bad, and ugly presidential leadership, the American military has weathered these storms time and time again. Politicians make decisions, generals build the plans, and soldiers execute (while grousing, of course). Decisions aren't perfect, plans fail, and soldiers deal with it. Such is war, a reality that can be tolerated when fallible presidents and generals make mistakes. Shit happens, but we hold our heads high. Historically, recruiting efforts have fluctuated with the economic health of the country—not the perception of the military. On balance, the modern-era military has done a solid (if very imperfect) job defending the nation and deterring gathering threats.

Not anymore.

As we approach the first full quarter of the twenty-first century—facing the most determined external enemy we've faced since Nazi Germany and the USSR—an even more dangerous internal trap has befallen our military. A domestic political cult of virtue-signaling, social justice saboteurs has targeted our military as the next trophy in their reckless big-game hunting of American traditions. This time, they're going straight for our immune system.

The results are self-evident. Our ongoing recruiting failures defy all past numbers. The military will make the excuse that three-fourths of American youth don't qualify for military service in the first place, but that's only part of the story. Why can't we entice the remainder of our young people—especially patriotic young men—to serve? As one active-duty Army colonel recently put it bluntly in an op-ed: "America fell out of love with its Army." He's right, especially regarding straight, white men—who represent both the largest portion of the force and the largest drop in recruitment. It's not a lack of recruiters, or a small recruiting budget. Both are larger than ever. And ongoing economic uncertainty, along with obscene college tuition costs, should be a recruiter's dream. Instead, Americans no longer trust their sons and daughters in the hands of Uncle Sam. Average Americans are smart, and see all the warning signs—the ism "days" ... the rainbow "flags" ... the forced "firsts" ... the fake "extremism" ... and the sheer failures. What do young people—and families—across America see that politicians and generals cannot? Or do our generals see the changes and accept them? The former is troubling; the latter is treasonous.

* * *

The Iraq War, like Vietnam, was hotly contested and vigorously protested, and has become the standard by which foolish wars of our generation are judged. I recoiled the first time I heard then-candidate Donald Trump call it a "stupid war" in 2015, but objectively he was right. The American political system is designed to recoil after unpopular foreign adventures—a healthy reflex. Following two terms of George W. Bush, and even after a successful tactical "surge" in Iraq, our country voted for "change." The country voted for political change—assuming that might change the conduct of the war, *but not the warriors themselves*. But a different kind of change came fast, and it started at the top.

What we didn't anticipate was the freak squad. Like a cartoonish circus, woke generals celebrate and promote people who their political masters tell they/them are "diverse." But the military isn't the Greatest Show, full of misfits, singing self-flattering numbers about how special they are. America is unique, in part, because we're free enough to tolerate misfits, but we won't stay that way if we make "misfit" the only acceptable identity. Normal dudes have always fought, and won, our wars. *Prove me wrong.*

A huge part of this existential threat to our fighting force lies in the type of personality we attract and promote into the general officer ranks. The promotion system has never been perfect—trust me, more on that later—but for over two hundred years, it has been largely based on one core tenet: *merit*. In recent years, certain commanders in chief have used promotions into the general officer ranks to exorcise the perceived racial, gender, and social demons of the past. *Quota first, quota often!* The sad truth is that abandoning merit-based promotions for social equity advancement only locks in a grievance culture. Hunting for racism, today's generals create racial strife. Pushing for gender equality, today's generals weaken unit readiness. Rooting out "extremism," today's generals push rank-and-file patriots out of their formations (I'm one of them). Embracing "trans" soldiers, today's generals walk on their own eggshells—instead of training up warriors. *Killers.* That's what they're supposed to do, right?

Rising to the rank of general—or chairman of the Joint Chiefs or secretary of defense—used to mean reaching the pinnacle of the "Profession of Arms." But not anymore. Starting largely under Obama, and again under Biden, reaching that level means a willingness to blindly impose social and political goals, the Constitution be damned. These men, and women, are cowards hiding under stars. *Whores to wokesters.* Wielding a transformative power that has undercut 250 years of success in training and executing combat readiness, these tin-plated bureaucrats exist to execute the perceived redemption for nineteenth-century America. They are willing tools, taking orders from Ivy League leftists who despise the institution they are supposed to be leading, but are instead betraying. Later, those pathetic generals retire, collect fat pensions, and sit on corporate defense boards. Cowards, then sellouts.

In 2008—in one of my first television appearances ever—I was on CNN's *Larry King Live* and debated former NATO Supreme Allied Commander General Wesley Clark about the war in Iraq. I was supporting the surge; he was against it. I was an Army first lieutenant; he was a retired four-star general and former NATO commander. *Who allowed that matchup? I hope someone on the Supreme Allied Commander's staff got an earful!* The general's understanding of his role in the Army was revealing, then and now.

General Clark said, "We had a million troops in Vietnam, 550,000 Americans, almost 500,000 from the Republic of Vietnam army. Plus, another million in uniform that were part of the local militia. And the more troops, the more casualties. Secondly, if you complain about the quality of the government, you're never going to solve this problem. We got rid of the government in Vietnam. We changed it, we still had problems. And to the end we complained that there was too much corruption."

My response to him that night was clear, but restrained: "With all due respect, General, you have taken off your 'general hat,' and put on a 'political hat.' The generals are not supposed to be politicians. The general's job is to fight and win the war when given the guidance from the commander in chief."

The general's comment was mostly benign political speech from a former commander now heavily involved in domestic partisan politics. He ran for president as a Democrat, after all. But it was a glimpse under the hood for a young junior officer. Our military can bounce back from bad military decisions from mediocre military leaders, but we can't bounce back from a radicalized military guided by the American equivalent of commissars—little Wesley Clarks at all ranks, pushing the latest political agendas instead of making merit-based, readiness-focused, military decisions. The influence of generals like Wesley Clark—and there are far worse—has been transformative inside the Pentagon. Unless things change, and fast, their social contagion will choke out more and more of the American fighting spirit.

This unholy alliance of political ideologues and Pentagon pussies has left our warriors without *real* defenders in Washington. Soldiers are either victims or villains, with the political class never taking responsibility for yesterday's vote. Our soldiers have never had that luxury. They simply serve and execute the commands given. Thankfully our history is filled with honorable soldiers who gave their all regardless of what the media and gilded classes thought of them.

African Americans fought in World War II before our armed forces were integrated, because their home country came first. America didn't deserve the humble devotion these incredible patriots displayed. It also happens that, as terrible as the racial discrimination that generation endured in our own nation, in 1941 the Nazis represented something far more evil and dangerous to human freedom. Had African Americans and other marginalized citizens not considered themselves of use to defending our nation at war, we may not have won. There would have been no *Brown v. Board of Education* ruling. There would have been no civil rights movement and no President Barack Obama (well, that one was a mistake).

African Americans furthered the cause of universal equality—*not equity*!—by serving selflessly in the armed forces at a time of war. Moreover, the courageous contributions of these patriotic Americans in the struggle against (real) fascism played a massive role in pushing back on the forces of racism within our own country. The case for desegregation had no real intellectual foil after World War II. All that was left was prejudice, stubbornness, and emotional paranoia. Dignity prevailed over ignorance. These stories never seem to find their way into African American History Month. Instead, the Left targets the very institutions that trailblazed the racial harmony they now seem so eager to prevent.

Pushing Critical Race Theory, undermining merit-based performance, convincing recruits to join the military for gender-reassignment treatment, pushing women into combat roles, prosecuting warfighters, targeting certain political persuasions, and new "green fleets" are *all* agendas being peddled by the Department of Defense's taxpayer-funded budget. They are all extraconstitutional and contrary to the dictates of a robust and ready military. They demand that the soldier genuflect to an ideology that is both foreign and antithetical to their own core beliefs.

The US military is not, and has never been, a partisan organization. We don't swear an oath to defend the flag or even the country. We don't have the authority to avenge specific wrongs or domestic grievances. Like our political representatives in Washington, DC, and in statehouses across the fruited plain, our oath is to protect and defend the Constitution of the United States of America against anyone who threatens it. The expectation is that we will defend it against all enemies—both foreign and domestic. Not political opponents, but real enemies. (Yes, Marxists are our enemies.)

Even if the modern Left has rejected this fact—and most youth are no longer taught it in school—without the Constitution we are not the United States of America. Like our Founders, we take our lessons from both ancient Israel and the Roman Republic. When we reject our covenants, religious or secular, when we malign our constitutional republic and its founding principles, we become a byword—and a curse to the world. A hypothetical *what went wrong* like so many dynasties of the past.

Busy killing Islamists in shithole countries—and then betrayed by our leaders—our warriors have every reason to let America's dynasty fade away. Leftists stole a lot from us, but we won't let them take this. Time for round two—we won't miss this war.

Chapter 2

EXTREMISTS THAT NEVER WERE

In February 2021, Secretary of Defense Lloyd Austin announced something big.

Through his then–Pentagon spokesman John Kirby, Austin ordered a one-day "stand-down" for all DoD personnel. A stand-down in the military is a total "relaxation of status of a military unit or force from an alert or operational posture"; simply put, you aren't a soldier, you are a student. You sit down in classes and learn not to do something someone else screwed up in the unit. DUI arrests deliver unit stand-downs. Sometimes the stand-down was for the company and not the entire battalion. Sometimes it was for an entire brigade, but not the division. Rare was the stand-down for the total active US Army, let alone the entire Department of Defense. What happened that the entire US military was being ordered to retrain and stand down?

This must be important.

Like, Boeing 737 Max recall important.

When the US Navy had a string of suicides in 2023, they had a two-day stand-down. When a helicopter crashed due to maintenance, there was a five-day stand-down. In this case, Secretary Austin ordered a military-wide stand-down. Every unit had sixty days to complete critical corrective training. For what?

"Extremism," of course.

Spokesman Kirby explained that akin to other military-wide pauses, "extremism" was of paramount urgency due to the events of January 6, 2021—which included a handful of active-duty soldiers and reservists entering the US Capitol.

In April of that year, Secretary Austin ordered his DoD to create what they called a "Countering Extremism Working Group," and the person they put in charge of that? A race-obsessed ideologue named Bishop Garrison, who would henceforth be the point of contact for all "extremist" subject matter, reporting directly to the secretary of defense.

This stand-down wasn't just for the active-duty forces in the DoD. Our service academies—West Point, Annapolis, Colorado Springs—were also pushed to transform the education of their alleged hateful hallways.

As easy as it would be to simply put all this woke drivel on the Biden administration, this fervor for ideological repentance did not start with Secretary Austin. It has also been a growing theme with the chairman of the Joint Chiefs of Staff, General Mark Milley, who was promoted to that role in 2018. A few years into the job, he suddenly discovered the ideological emergency of rampant racism in the ranks. In July 2020, in the aftermath of the George Floyd incident, Secretary of Defense Mark Esper (whom President Trump later fired), with General Milley's approval, ordered that all photographs be removed from consideration of promotion boards and selection processes to emphasize Diversity, Equity, and Inclusion. Without saying it explicitly, his order implied that, previously, if a commander or a promotion board saw a skin color that was different than their own, then senior leaders in the United States military—who for twenty years delivered folded flags to grieving families representing all races, creeds, religions, sexualities, and socioeconomic backgrounds—would not promote a qualified soldier due to their skin tone. This was absurd on its face—outrageous to *think* about our great institution, let alone write out and disseminate.

If this were a real problem that military leaders believed existed, then surely these duty-bound officers would have resigned and stated openly why they were leaving. They'd say something like, "This military is not promoting people because of skin color, and I can't lead, nor will I be a part of an organization that conducts itself in a manner that I believe is racist." That's how you get on the cover of *Time* magazine and get a segment at the Academy Awards. Like all abuses, the calling out of specific examples of abuse is critically important to showing both the problem and its unapologetic solution. That would send the message.

But of course that never happened. These leaders wanted to agree with the trendy 2020 belief that all institutions were thoroughly, insidiously racist, without needing to prove that it was true. So they went looking to solve problems that didn't actually exist. A problem *they knew* did not exist. Such virtue signaling isn't harmless, however. These performative self-flagellations signal to average men and women in the military that leaders care more about media attention than actual problems and people. Worse, by peddling the lie of racism in the military—which they knowingly did—they sully the reputation of an institution they purport to lead.

* * *

Good leaders know their subordinates. They have a finger on the pulse of their culture. Bad leaders follow the political winds. Surely, a man who has been in the Army for forty-three years would have identified this supposed problem of massive military systemic racism before George Floyd was killed. Mark Milley never complained about racism in the ranks in the 1990s. Or the 2000s. Or the 2010s. Then suddenly, in 2020, racism was everywhere. If racism in the military is so bad, then Milley was willfully blind about it for decades. Or he was racist. Or he is lying today. I vote for the latter.

Yet General Milley felt this was so important that he and Secretary Esper issued guidance on this topic a month after the nation was divided by racial unrest. As American cities burned that summer in 2020, our Department of Defense leadership, still sour over a photo of their commander in chief holding a Bible defiantly outside the White House, chose this time to address what they perceived as problems of "equity" in their ranks. Everything about it was virtue signaling absent any real impact, genuflecting at the altar of Black Lives Matter (BLM) orthodoxy.

It was reflexive as much as it was pandering. This was absurd guidance. The department updated its already ironclad policies against racism to bolster protections for soldiers against inappropriate and intolerable harassing behaviors, especially racial bias and prejudice. But it was not enough that General Milley and Secretary Esper stopped the abuse that they claimed existed in *their* force (but without ever calling out specific people acting in an unbecoming manner). They covered their own posteriors by claiming that these abuses are not always transparent. Stealth. Which means you can't see it, but we must be on watch to stop it.

The ghostly threat of racism. It is never a good idea to give an authoritarian, command-centered organization the ability to punish thought crimes without evidence of actual criminal damage. Trump would call it a witch hunt, and he would be right. And once this race obsession took hold, it only grew—mostly unabated to this day.

Secretary Esper then released the official Department of Defense Board on Diversity and Inclusion Report Recommendations to Improve Racial and Ethnic Diversity and Inclusion in the U.S. Military. In Appendix E, the determination was made that even hairstyles are discriminatory. And the DoD should loosen its standards with regards to beards, wigs, and hair styles to promote—you guessed it—Diversity, Equity, and Inclusion. When I was in the Army, we kicked out good soldiers for having naked women tattooed on their arms and today we are relaxing the standards on shaving, dreadlocks, man buns, and straight-up obesity. Piece by piece, the standards had to go . . . because of equity.

The religion of woke Marxist policies didn't start—or stop—with the soldiers in the field. Tattoos, hairstyles, language, and genders are just one part of the woke road. To transform military culture into woke culture, you need to indoctrinate officers. You need to get to them early, and that means you intercept them when they first join the military. That would come next.

Not all Congress sat on their hands and bit their tongue. Tennessee representative Republican Mark Green, a combat veteran himself, issued a press release in May 2021 announcing a bill to ban DEI and CRT in our military. Representative Green said,

> *Critical Race Theory is based on a massive and purposeful misunderstanding of the American founding, American history, and America as it exists today. This is a Marxist ideology created to tear American institutions down. It teaches Americans and members of the Armed Services to judge one another by the color of their skin instead of by the "content of their character." America should never*

go back to this kind of thinking. The United States military service academies are designed to train leaders and warriors for combat— men and women of every race, creed, and religion. Critical Race Theory's divisiveness will destroy the unit cohesion necessary to win in combat and defend this nation.

He's right, of course, but nobody listened.

Just a month before Green introduced that bill, General Mark Milley, the chairman of the Joint Chiefs of Staff—the same position he held under President Trump when these initiatives creeped their way out of the shadows—testified at a congressional budget hearing regarding the 2022 defense budget along with Secretary of Defense Austin.

Representative Matt Gaetz, a Republican from Florida, asked Secretary Austin about Critical Race Theory and if it was being advanced in the DoD. Austin shocked the room when he stated categorically,

We do not teach critical race theory. We don't embrace critical race theory, and I think that's a spurious conversation. We are focused on extremist behaviors and not ideology—not people's thoughts, not people's political orientation. Behaviors is what we're focused on.

A political answer, from a seasoned politician with stars on his shoulder.

General Mark Milley was more honest. Obviously not seeing the irony in interrupting the black secretary of defense, Lloyd Austin, Milley pushed aside his self-awareness and interrupted the SecDef. He defended the CRT policies that his Senate-confirmed secretary of defense just denied. Milley went on to talk about how his force needed to understand all extremist behavior to understand why it is bad. He said,

I've read Mao Zedong. I've read Karl Marx. I've read Lenin. That doesn't make me a communist. So what is wrong with understanding—having some situational understanding about the country for which we are here to defend? . . . I want to understand white rage, and I'm white, and I want to understand it.

Milley almost did it. He almost said he read Hitler, but he kept that name far from the performance art he was conducting. Milley clearly believes that to understand why this nation was and always has been worthy of blood and sacrifice, we must first fully understand the point of view of our communist and fascist enemies. Think about that for a second. This isn't some confused ROTC-grad Tanker that a reporter asked to wish his family back home a Merry Christmas and who said something accidentally stupid or controversial on live television. This was a forty-three-year officer, who is the chairman of the Joint Chiefs of Staff, stating that to have "some situational understanding about the country for which we are here to defend" he first needs to do a deep dive into the ideology of our enemy. Does this imply that if Marx, Stalin, or Lenin raise a valid point in their communist thinking, maybe he will think twice about the 0200 bombardment that would lead to defeating these same communist enemies in future wars? And as far as "white rage," does that mean soldiers should similarly be informed of the intricacies of racist tomes like *The Protocols of the Elders of Zion*? It's absurd.

This was maddening.

Regardless of his naughty summer reading list, one of the core problems of General Milley's soliloquy was that the DoD was not discussing or researching "white rage." They were *accusing* their members of "white rage" and consigning them to reeducation classes to cure them of their perceived wrongdoings. One does not need a sixty-day stand-down to dispatch a few officers to the local university to acquaint oneself with such widespread and popular leftist ideological opinions. And do we really think they needed a graduate-level course in the history of white supremacy? No, something else was inspiring the general to get so fired up.

> *And I personally find it offensive that we are accusing the United States military, our general officers, our commissioned, noncommissioned officers of being, quote, "woke" or something else, because we're studying some theories that are out there.*
>
> *I want to understand white rage, and I'm white, and I want to understand it. So, what is it that caused thousands of people to assault this building and try to overturn the Constitution of the United States of America? What caused that? I want to find that out.*

And just like that, we got our answer: January 6. This was all about January 6, 2021. At least that was the convenient answer given by Biden DoD officials under General Mark Milley.

From the presence of a few active-duty service members at the Capitol these officials had extrapolated to a service-wide problem necessitating a full shutdown. For the record, when academics actually got around to asking real soldiers, they found that "veterans expressed much lower support for White supremacists than the U.S. population overall (0.7 percent versus 7 percent)" as well as lower "support for Antifa than the overall U.S. population (5.5 percent versus 10 percent)."[*] The Biden administration's own investigation found only 100 cases of extremist activity among

---

[*] Rand Corporation, "Support for Extremism Among U.S. Military Veterans Is Similar to Public at Large," press release, May 23, 2023, https://www.rand.org/news/press/2023/05/23.html.

2.1 million active and reserve forces, "a case rate of .005 percent."* Another DoD-led study in January 2024 confirms all this as well.† Turns out the military is *less racist and less extreme* than the US population. That was a fact, and is a fact. If you ask any veteran of the past forty years—except Mark Milley, of course—they would tell you that. Before, or after, January 6 or the 2020 so-called "summer of love."

So how out of touch do military leaders have to be to misunderstand the nature of their command so profoundly? Consider that this was the same General Mark Milley who created the Naming Commission in charge of renaming nine evil military bases with confederate names at a cost of $21 million, before his team realized that they needed more tax money and adjusted the total to $39 million. The same man who—years before—commanded two of those bases at Fort Bragg and Fort Hood and never once, not one time, raised the issue that commanding forces at bases named after a racist Confederate general could be bad for morale.

When Milley was in charge of Fort Hood years ago, he didn't seem offended by its name. Then he didn't care to use his rank to display leadership and change. Milley didn't waste his time displaying curiosity about other points of view. He knew nothing about racism. This only became an issue in 2021. Back then he understood American history to a point and seemed to believe that leaders lead and are not controlled by past failures. Then his mission was war and allegedly fighting to win the war. Back then Mark Milley was different. He did PT.

* Marco Rubio and Chip Roy, *Woke Warriors: How Political Ideology Is Weakening America's Military*, https://www.rubio.senate.gov/wp-content/uploads/_cache/files/ee1d7a86-6d0c-4f08-bd15-24e5b28e54b7/3756824FA9C21B819BB97AAB16221530.woke-warfighters-report-3.pdf.

† Kristina Wong, "Study Found No 'Extremism' Problem in the Military, Despite Biden Administration's Narrative," Breitbart, January 4, 2024, https://www.breitbart.com/politics/2024/01/04/study-found-no-extremism-problem-in-the-military-despite-biden-administrations-narrative/.

Yet today, with different pressure, coming from different political leaders, Milley spent $40 million to stop this national nightmare before one more day was spent with these old names on military bases. He survived the racist bases, but others mustn't endure such horrid racism!

America and her military should be grateful that General Milley and Secretary Austin had diagnosed the problem. But who would save our nation from her racist military?

* * *

To fight racist extremism, you obviously need an extreme partisan who sees every disagreement as being racism. You need a professional racist. His name was Bishop Garrison. Garrison said this about President Trump and his supporters on Twitter back in July 2019.

> *Silence from our Congressional leaders is complicity. (Trump) is only going to get worse from here, & his party and its leadership are watching it happen while doing nothing to stop it. Support for him, a racist, is support for ALL his beliefs.*
>
> *(Trump's) dragging a lot of bad actors (misogynist, extremists, other racists) out into the light, normalizing their actions. If you support the President, you support that. There is no room for nuance with this. There is no more "but I'm not like that" talk.*
>
> *Because you're watching what (Trump) says. You're listening to his careful choice of words. And you're still willing to follow him and/or not speak out. So yes, you're very much like that. It's time we all step up. #WeArePatriots #Black44*

I can't blame civilian leaders for having partisan axes to grind. They always have and always will. The true outrage is not that there are politicians who want to bend America's military to fit their radical racial ideology; the real outrage is that the military is in on it. Men in camouflage allowed this to happen twenty short years after September 11. The military allowed it. I allowed it. *You did nothing.*

They were doing to soldiers all over this military what Arthur Miller wrote about in the classic play *The Crucible*. In a classic witch hunt formulation, they created a straw man of their own design, hung a banner around its neck with the word Trump on it, and then let loose the dogs of war.

They found a willing participant in Bishop Garrison. Garrison was a former Army officer with deployments in the Middle East. That checked the box of why he was at the Pentagon. In 2021 he was given the title of DoD "Human Capital, Diversity, Equity and Inclusion senior advisor." Garrison is a self-described full-throated advocate of Critical Race Theory. Of course, there is nothing wrong with that in a free country . . . unless you are arguing, as his sitting secretary of defense, Lloyd Austin, had just testified under oath to Congress, that there was no CRT in the DoD.

Bishop Garrison, the man the DoD brought in to advise them on all things DEI, believes that all American history can be explained by "racial oppression." He was an outspoken supporter of the Marxist 1619 Project, which, peer-reviewed history papers agree, was wildly biased and inaccurate. This same *New York Times*–launched 1619 Project was what Garrison believed should be infused into the Department of Defense.

In April 2021, he was put in charge of the Countering Extremism Working Group (CEWG) stand-down to address military extremism. A man who called "white supremacy the greatest threat to the U.S. military" and that white nationalist extremism were "nation-ending threats

unless the government invests in combating violent extremist programs."
Yep, this is going to end well.

This would be radical enough for a host at MSNBC, but this guy was in charge of evaluating the Uniformed Code of Military Justice (UCMJ) and determining who was a threat to the nation's future. He would oversee vetting soldiers by looking at their social media to find signs of extremist behavior and determining whether they were fit to serve or fit for promotion.

A *real* bigot was in charge of vetting nonracists whom he/they did not agree with politically. This was about purging supporters of President Donald J. Trump. During the first impeachment of Trump, Bishop Garrison said that those calling for civility were "the death of this nation."

A year before becoming the DoD racism czar, Garrison argued for "tearing down [Immigration and Customs Enforcement] to the studs so you never hear ICE in government again" and that the United States couldn't ever again make the claim to be a beacon of liberty, justice, and freedom anywhere in the world so long as it was acceptable to condone "the ongoing murder of innocent black people." Our enemies have literally used Garrison's vitriol against us in bilateral negotiations with our own State Department. A year later, while National Security Advisor Jake Sullivan was confronting Chinese leaders on their recent cyberattacks on Hong Kong and Taiwan, Chinese Communist Party officials quoted Garrison about not being able to dictate liberty to the world.

So why would anyone want to place a man who believes his own nation should destroy its nuclear arsenal, or believes that America is "undemocratic, slavery-based" and could say aloud in a room full of military leaders as he did in 2021 that the president of the United States has a "constitutional responsibility to confront climate change," in the position to make universal changes to military policy or conduct?

Maybe it's because he simply reflects his military leadership. It was General Mark Milley, after all, who commissioned a report from the U.S. Army War College on the implications of climate change and advanced the idea of service academies offering more courses on Critical Race Theory.

Ultimately, all of this comes down to how we define extremism. People like you and me picture suicide bombers. Bishop Garrison envisions . . . people like you and me. Domestic opponents are far worse than genuine terrorists.

If you support Trump, and supporting Trump makes you a racist and extreme, then in the world of Bishop Garrison, you are a de facto extremist. No nuance. No question. No quarter. In the end, it isn't about white supremacy or white nationalism. Those views and tattoos have been banned in the military for a long time. If I had a white supremacist or racist in my infantry platoon I could, and would, kick them out. It would be my duty and my pleasure to do it. But I didn't have to. Because it wasn't an issue. I served with black, brown, and white soldiers. All I ever saw was Army green.

That's what the Army taught me. And that is how I led my men. But for Bishop Garrison all he sees is red. MAGA Red. But Pete, you say, this is just a committee to study extremism not political persuasion. Oh really? Think again, it actually gets worse. In March 2022, a leaked seventeen-page DARPA presentation—DARPA is the Pentagon's research lab—marked unclassified, outlined extremism and insider threats in the DoD. The document is very startling, and would be resource material for Bishop Garrison. It's the type of fertile DoD cultural soil he is standing on right now. Not only does this document assert that extremism is rampant in the military, but it suggests a new form of extremism I've never heard of in the military called . . . Patriot Extremism.

What?

If you want an effective military, your target recruiting constituency is . . . patriots. They're not on your enemy list. Unless the purge is coming.

The Left—Bishop Garrison and his DEI disciples—saw their opening. They had the power, and unlimited avenues to virtue-signal. They had their men in the right places. They told us—without evidence but *with* a parroting press corps—that extremism was a huge military problem. They said Trump supporters are extremists, full stop. So where does that leave Trump supporters, patriots, and conservatives in the military today? Vetted. Closeted. Or worse, *kicked out.* The Left knew, and knows, that the military is one of the last traditional, aggressive, value-based organizations in America. So they had to dismantle it—and now was their moment.

The military has always been about social engineering—forging young men (mostly) with skills, discipline, pride, and a brotherhood. It takes average American boys, breaks down their body and mind, and builds them back up into members of a warfighting team. It changes the way they view the world. Men and women gain perspective, toughness, self-reliance, but also teamwork. They learn dedication to the Constitution, and commitment to a code of honor. Some carry rifles, others program radios, others drive trucks, and others fix those trucks. The military—properly understood—changes lives.

No wonder the Left wanted to get their hands on it so badly.

Come to think of it, the Department of Defense—before the full-out assault from the Obama and Biden administrations—was the last bastion of meritocracy in America. You can buy your kid's way into Harvard or Yale. The media is full of nepotism, and mediocrity. And government is crony as hell, from top to bottom. But a spot in the military, for the most part, is earned. Especially in elite units. The Navy SEALs don't care who your dad is, or how much money you make. Neither do the Green Berets nor the Marines. The military, properly understood, forges future leaders with fidelity to the Constitution—from the small-town poor kid to the big-city rich kid.

That makes it very dangerous to the Left. How can a political force that wants to shred the Constitution and abhors meritocracy tolerate an entire department of government—the largest department—that believes the exact opposite? It can't. Hence why Obama, harboring a famous distrust of military generals, started to remake the Pentagon in his image.

First, he staffed top civilian defense positions with like-minded left-wing political appointees. Then he started rewarding—and promoting—generals and admirals who were willing to kowtow to those ideologues. Generals who did not follow the Obama line were admonished, sidelined, or fired. As such, the signal was sent down the ranks: comply with the new social justice priorities or your career is toast. So, for eight years—and now for four more years under Biden—the pipelines of future military leaders have been primed with social justice, politically correct parrots. Parrots who love "firsts" instead of fighters. Puppets who will spout "our diversity is our strength" when they know damn well that it's the opposite in the military: our unity is our strength. They are dangerous idiots, and they are in charge.

Pretty soon, you have a military that no longer socially engineers united patriots, but instead is intended to filter out, dilute, and sideline patriots—consequences be damned. And tells troops that their individual differences are what define them, and make them special. Just like academia, media, social media, major corporations, and Hollywood, the Left is obsessed with controlling everything—and the military is the crown jewel.

But the problem is bigger than the Left. It lies in changes that have taken place, invisibly, in the culture around us. Assumptions about men, about warriors, about honor. Taking back the military will require attacking those assumptions by remembering the best of who we are.

Chapter 3

COWBOYS LED BY COWARDS

Americans used to *love* cowboys. Now they seem like a quaint part of our past. We used to see the dignity and value of men who got up early, made real things, lived by a code, and worked with their hands. Cowboys were our heroes, as were soldiers, explorers, and astronauts. Now? It's Tony Fauci and Michelle Obama who get the hero treatment. Careerist media-types only recognize so-called elite people like themselves.

There's an old western that's about a conflict between two types of gunslingers. One of them is bitter and greedy, mad at the world for not giving him what he's owed. He can see success only in terms of monetary gain. "You know what's on the back of a poor man when he dies? The clothes of pride," he grumbles. "Is that all you want?"

His friend replies, "All I want is to enter my house justified." He has his eye on a far more powerful sort of fulfillment than his bitter friend can understand.

Something that you're not likely to hear much about in today's "civilized," safety-obsessed world is the idea of honor. Our elites talk about it like it's an archaic value, a holdover from medieval barbarism. Feminists and leftists assume that honor is just a façade for fragile-ego bullies. For *toxic* men of yesteryear. In their mind, sane people don't take real risks for something as intangible as their personal reputation, their faith, or a cause for their country.

Yet we start to lose *everything* when people won't risk *anything* to defend something besides money, power, or status. We become selfish and focused only on shallow, worldly achievements. Vocations that are less financially rewarding but offer lots of meaning to life are disdained in a post-honor culture.

That's why being a veteran no longer demands respect of the coastal elites or reverence from large swaths of the public. The media and so-called elite institutions portray soldiers as thoughtless, order-following grunts. They envision the "elite" of society as those who go into the bureaucracy, the media, or the political realm, which means that those who enter the military and work with their hands are not elite. According to them, serving in the military may be a nice vocation for the lower class, but that's all it is.

In previous generations, men had to find ways to salvage their honor if they *didn't* get to fight in a war. Think George Bailey in *It's a Wonderful Life*, bitterly stuck at home. He's haunted by the worry that his life is insignificant. As I recount in my first book—*In the Arena*—a stoic Vietnam veteran told me at nineteen years old, "Pete, whatever you do, don't miss your war."

As I recall, "The stark statement ricocheted around my brain like a stray bullet. I knew nothing of the military—let alone war. I was not from a military family, and couldn't tell you the difference between the Army and the Marine Corps. While I was captivated by our lunch conversation, it was not what I expected to hear . . . He said it with certainty that I had yet to hear in my short life, except from a pulpit. (And they didn't teach that in church.)

"To my virgin ears, he sounded cavalier. Was he a warmonger? Or was he just crazy? America was not [yet] at war, so I immediately dismissed it—but I never forgot it. Years later, not until I got back from Iraq in 2006 and then out the ass end of the political wringer in 2008, did I finally understand his point—and agree with it. For that veteran, his statement was not just about Vietnam, it was not about the rightness or wrongness of that war, and it certainly was not about a naked thirst for war. Through those four words—*don't miss your war*—he spoke of honor. Of duty. Of courage. Of God and country. Of the arena. Like an evangelical preacher of America's civil religion—and like Teddy Roosevelt—he had been to the arena, and was urging me."

He was a cowboy—who entered his house justified.

Today, especially for coastal elites, a history of military service is a passive-aggressive mark *against* a man. *You did what? You must be messed up. What a waste . . . and the wars went terribly!* This inversion has jettisoned a lot of attributes that virtuous men used to covet: honor, selflessness, courage, integrity. Instead, these values are replaced with optics-obsessed performativity, selfish careerism, effeminacy, and duplicity.

Like so many civic perversions, this way of thinking started in the progressive era, when many of our political leaders saw themselves as elite "thinkers." The most famous progressive elite was President Woodrow Wilson, the Princeton president who became governor of New Jersey and then president of the United States. President Wilson was not one to follow the Constitution; why should he follow something that he considered below his own abilities and reason?

Men like Wilson were "subject matter experts." They were the "best and the brightest," and they earned their position at the top, not because they were great warriors or rock-ribbed men, but because they were the most "intellectual." (During the progressive era Teddy Roosevelt was the only president who served—and he got the Medal of Honor.) The spoils, starting in that era and among the self-appointed elite "experts," no longer went to the fastest and the strongest, but to the new intellectual masters; the new leaders were the educated, chattering classes. They deserved their place at the top of the food chain, martial values be damned.

For this group, what separated the constitutional from the monstrous was how they saw "their peer group"—and then those who were outside their rigid lines of demarcation. For racists like Wilson and FDR, the "other" were their own nonwhite citizens. Why should they respect the constitutional rights of those who don't look or think like they did? No wonder these men imprisoned inconvenient protestors, arrested journalists, denied awards, interned Asian Americans, and experimented on minorities in the military.

Under the leadership of politicians who believed that they were the enlightened class, the military was seen as the blunt instrument of the king. No longer were warriors the defenders of the Republic; they were instead dull and dim-witted creatures incapable of intellectual maturity. In later years, this type of thinking was shared by Vietnam medal tosser and presidential candidate Senator John Kerry, who famously said on the importance of education that if "you make an effort to be smart, you can do well. If you don't, you get stuck in Iraq." No surprise that Kerry is from the same party as Wilson and Roosevelt—all Democrats.

The traditional understanding of the agrarian soldier citizen, who picked up arms to defend his nation as a citizen, was rejected by the progressive elites. They believed that only suckers get drafted and go to war.

Later, this same group posited that people volunteered only for socioeconomic reasons. "Take a look at the Marines—what you see is black faces, from the ghettos," said Noam Chomsky in the 1980s. "Sometime in the seventies, the American army shifted to a traditional mercenary army of the poor." You can hear the contempt for these patriotic Americans. Poor. Black. Clearly, they have to be exploited victims.

"There is no such thing as a 'volunteer army,'" he said. He simply couldn't comprehend that decent American men who weren't shaped by upper-class fashions would want to serve America because they loved the country. Small-minded Chomsky assumed they were out to make a buck. Or just to pay for tuition.

Decades after Vietnam, Senator Kerry was still "stuck" in the thinking that if you left college, the only way for an unskilled working man to make a living was to serve in the military, and then in foolish wars. Soldiering was a last resort for the desperate and rudderless proletariat.

The Beltway crowd sees the military as hopelessly regressive and unnecessary. As their New World Order comes into focus the need for a muscular military has become less necessary, and less desirable. Furthermore, if the problem of modern violence is defined as the Western White Male mindset (American values of federalism, capitalism, and Western-Christian constitutionalism) then once we dismantle the American Way, the need to protect and defend the Constitution and its citizens falls by the wayside.

Sadly, this type of thinking, which used to be considered madness, has become the fundamental assumption of those who wish to defund the police, co-opt the military, and criminalize differences in political opinions. If the bad guys (our enemies) are just misinterpreted freedom fighters (of any stripe), then the good guys can stand down the military and bend to the inevitable "arc of history"—one of the lamest progressive phrases out there. You see, the good guys (progressives) always win, and they (progressives) are always the good guys. *In their own minds.* Progressives can't imagine the need for a military because they assume we'll conquer every problem through the values of godless and false empathy, inclusion, and coexistence. Not that we even need to defeat external enemies, because progressives are confident that the real problem is their fellow citizens who won't bend the knee to their god of government power and "social justice." It is easy for the Left to worship false gods when they do not accept the existence of any real God.

But, hey, maybe forcing noncommissioned officers to don fake breasts and plastic "empathy bellies" during training to understand how pregnant women feel—as the Army did in 2012 (under Obama's "transformation")—will help these guys kick some terrorist ass. You know. Empathetically.

Is the goal of the military to suppress natural masculine instincts for honor and competition and replace them with empathy and plastic breasts? This was 2012, and it has not gotten better. Today's military wants pregnant woman—for "equity's" sake—to be combatant commanders! *Don't you know that pregnant nonbinary women are killers too!?* To the Left, the real enemies are commonsense Americans who reject this nonsense.

Meanwhile, fighting the wrong domestic enemies has signaled weakness to the real ones outside our borders. Under Commander in Chief Joe Biden, America's generals have ceded ground—or outright defeat—on every contested battlespace with a foreign adversary. We lost Afghanistan, giving the Taliban nine military bases at a cost of hundreds of billions of dollars. Billions of wasted dollars on armor, helicopters, biometric scanning equipment, and intelligence-gathering tools that they now use on their own people—and sell to our enemies. Russia has had its way in Eastern Europe. Iran moves on Israel, most brutally through Hamas on October 7, 2023. China is on the edge of dominating its geographic neighbors, especially Taiwan. North Korea taunts and bullies at will. And our southern border is wide open to any adversary with a plan and some plane tickets. America is less safe, and our generals simply do not care about the oath that they swore to uphold. The generals are too busy assessing how domestic "extremists" wearing Carhartt jackets will usurp our "democracy" with gate barriers or flagpoles.

* * *

This brings me to a simple question.

Why can't we just fire the generals who have failed?

One warrant officer in the U.S. Army Special Forces, Brad Paul—who has thirteen combat deployments under his belt—told me this: "The current state of the military is careerism. It no longer centers on our core task: to win wars. Indeed, the ethos is: Where's my next command? How am I going to advance myself? That pushes our leaders toward protecting careers and we never filter out the turds."

Careerism is about winning, but only personally. You can't win a war if every soldier's out for himself, and *especially* if a leader is so focused on covering his ass that he can't be honest about failure. Today's military lacks a core value from our leadership that we all demand of every soldier that serves. *Integrity*. At the highest levels of command, they're not living up to our core values. I heard it from every soldier I spoke with for this book, dozens and dozens. They don't agree on everything. But the one thing they do agree on is that US military leadership has an integrity and accountability problem.

We can't think about winning the next big war if we aren't honest about the failures of the past. Our generals are not ready for this moment in history. Not even close. The next president of the United States needs to radically overhaul Pentagon senior leadership to make us ready to defend our nation and defeat our enemies. Lots of people need to be fired.

The debacle in Afghanistan, of course, is the most glaring example.

On August 26, 2021, thirteen Americans were killed and 170 Afghans died when an ISIS-K suicide bomber detonated outside the Abbey Gate at Karzai (now Kabul) International Airport during the humiliating retreat from Afghanistan. Three days later, American military leadership boasted that they took out a cell of ISIS-K that plotted and commanded the bombing at Abbey Gate. The *New York Times* later revealed that the American retaliatory attack killed ten innocent Afghans, seven of whom were children. The Pentagon confirmed the report. Our leaders at the Pentagon botched security (turns out the Taliban aren't our friends), cocked up the retreat, lost thirteen soldiers in a preventable security breach, and then lied to the world. The US killed a family in Kabul—and for four days claimed it was a "righteous strike." They knew it wasn't, almost right away. To revive a modified Iraq War slogan, "People died, Biden lied."

There was no accountability for the attack that killed Americans or for the "retaliatory" strike. The same leaders who lied about killing a family of ten were the same leaders who turned over security for Karzai International Airport to the Taliban. How in the hell do you think ISIS was allowed to leak through and kill thirteen American warriors? Who put the lives of our troops in the hands of the Taliban? Who thought it was a good idea to close Bagram Air Base, and then evacuate? Who thought we should leave all our equipment behind? Who prevented our Marines from shooting anyone that looked like a threat (and some Marines believe they had the suicide bomber in their sights, but were not allowed to engage)? And then lied about killing innocent civilians to cover their ass?

In a rare show of journalistic integrity, if not for the *New York Times*, we would have never known that the DoD actually killed a UN worker whose crime was delivering potable water along with seven children. It took weeks before US generals admitted their mistake.

These generals lied. They mismanaged. They violated their oath. They failed. They disgraced our troops, and our nation. They got people killed, unnecessarily. And, to this moment, they keep their jobs. Worse, they continue to actively erode our military and its values—by capitulating to civilians with radical agendas. They are an embarrassment, with stars still on their shoulders.

These generals are doing to our soldiers what progressives have always done. They give them experimental injections, they use them as social experiments, they throw them into harm's way without a clear plan, and then they insult them when they complain of lost comrades and shattered souls.

We are led by cowards, in and out of uniform.

When these shattered souls invoke a constitutional defense, on any number of matters, they are told they surrendered their constitutional rights. Soldiers do not surrender constitutional rights when they join the service, just as politicians do not surrender them in joining Congress.

This type of thinking makes it easy for the political class to think that the soldier's job is to just follow the orders of civilian leadership. It is not. Our military men and women take an oath that is very similar to the oaths taken by every branch of government and every civil servant. The oath is as follows . . .

> I, _____, do solemnly swear (or affirm) that I will support and defend the Constitution of the United States against all enemies, foreign and domestic; that I will bear true faith and allegiance to the same; and that I will obey the orders of the President of the United States and the orders of the officers appointed over me, according

to regulations and the Uniform Code of Military Justice. So help me God.

We do not take an oath solely to follow the orders of the president or solely to follow the orders of our leadership. Our first and foremost understanding as soldiers is that we, alongside every other member of government, fight to protect and defend the Constitution of the United States against all enemies, foreign and domestic.

The oath of office—an oath I took and administered many times in uniform—does not ask the soldier to surrender to the Congress any more than it asks the judge to surrender to the executive branch of government. It demands that each man and woman give themselves over to the sacred commitment that is chiseled into the Constitution of the United States of America. We don't surrender to a branch of government, a politician, or a party. We serve the constitutional order to which we have sworn our allegiance.

Soldiers do this despite their disdain for the civilian "elite" classes—because they know that real threats can't be wished away with kumbaya ideology or DEI consultants.

There is something all these woke, CRT/DEI professional contrarians in the Pentagon are missing. American exceptionalism is not due to our tribe, our whiteness, our wealth, or our land. The Russians, Germans, and the English have a longer and deeper white-dominated culture than America ever had. There are more obvious Christian empires like the Holy Roman Empire, Spanish Conquistadors—who had slaves in America a full one hundred years before the English colonialists, and England in the nineteenth century. If this issue was about land or wealth, then we can easily acknowledge that as far as territory goes, Mexico and South America are functionally as bountiful territorially as the continental United States.

America is exceptional because of our freedom-based, faith-infused form of government. First our principled Declaration of Independence, and then our codified Constitution, are what has made us distinct, durable, and righteous. Our Constitution was forged over the debates of great philosophical thinkers who, like "iron sharpens iron," clashed over the roles of the state, human nature, and the sovereignty of the people. They acknowledged the sinfulness of fallen humanity and erected spheres of governmental authority that checked the strength and power of the other spheres. They separated the branches of government so that power might be shared and authority splintered, in order to maximize the freedom of individuals. They allowed the Constitution to be amended but placed enough resistance in the system to make sure that amendments were not easily forced upon the nation by a wave of hysteria.

Our Founders understood how fragile the entire experiment is—as Benjamin Franklin famously said, when asked what type of government we had, "a Republic, if you can keep it."

* * *

You might ask, why did a chapter about military leadership devolve into a polemic on the Constitution? Because, if we are to revive this Republic, it starts with first principles. Today, we have a general-class divorced from this truth. They serve other masters. They serve ideological politicians, upside-down regulations, Ivy League graduate degrees, and opportunistic defense contractors. The next president of the United States needs to fire them all—or at least most of them—and install leaders with real fidelity to the Constitution. Black, white, male, female—none of that shit matters. "Firsts" don't matter. Who you have sex with doesn't matter. The only thing that matters is first principles, courageous leadership, laser focus on readiness, and the ability and willingness to exact lethality.

The fact that our culture no longer sees soldiering as a high-class vocation is a side effect of the same philosophy that creates feckless generals. We've abandoned an honor culture for a victim culture. The values we promote now are about self-flagellation, not taking responsibility. We envision a world without agency, where people are buffeted by forces of oppression and privilege, instead of being able to be heroes or villains on their own merits.

We need to clean house of woke generals. Currently the Department of Defense has forty-four four-star generals with a total force of 1.2 million serving. In World War II, there were only seven four-star generals and over 21 million were serving. It's upside down, and ripe for firings— without replacements.

A military think tank called the Quincy Institute for Responsible Statecraft found that twenty-six of the thirty-two four-star officers who retired after June 2018 were employed by defense contractors. That's 80 percent in the last five years. The military-industrial complex has been busy, and effective.

The Quincy Institute concluded in its October 2023 report something obvious: that when generals do this it "generates the appearance— and in some cases the reality—of conflicts of interest in the making of defense policy and in the shaping of the size and composition of the Pentagon budget."

Here's some common sense that would go a long way. If elected officials can't lobby Congress for a period of time after they retire or are voted out, why should generals move from their comfy desk jobs in the Pentagon to the boardroom of the military-industrial complex? Dwight D. Eisenhower warned specifically about this in his farewell address as president in 1961.

Our military organization today bears little relation to that known by any of my predecessors in peacetime, or indeed by the fighting men of World War II or Korea. Until the latest of our world conflicts, the United States had no armaments industry. American makers of plowshares could, with time and as required, make swords as well. But now we can no longer risk emergency improvisation of national defense; we have been compelled to create a permanent armaments industry of vast proportions. Added to this, three and a half million men and women are directly engaged in the defense establishment. We annually spend on military security more than the net income of all United State corporations.

This conjunction of an immense military establishment and a large arms industry is new in the American experience. The total influence—economic, political, even spiritual—is felt in every city, every state house, every office of the Federal government. We recognize the imperative need for this development. Yet we must not fail to comprehend its grave implications. Our toil, resources and livelihood are all involved; so is the very structure of our society.

In the councils of government, we must guard against the acquisition of unwarranted influence, whether sought or unsought, by the military-industrial complex. The potential for the disastrous rise of misplaced power exists and will persist.

We must never let the weight of this combination endanger our liberties or democratic processes. We should take nothing for granted. Only an alert and knowledgeable citizenry can compel the proper meshing of the huge industrial and military machinery of defense with our peaceful methods and goals, so that security and liberty may prosper together.

Truer today than ever before. Might this be why we buy F35s and they need new engines three years later? Or why our Army rolls out electric-powered Humvees when they know the entire exercise is political bullshit? Or why we sell artillery to Ukraine when we know our stockpile is depleted?

Modern American generals don't care that the Taliban are selling our equipment everywhere—including to Hamas—because, newly minted on the board of Raytheon, they will just sign another deal with their three-star general buddy and buy more equipment to give away to our enemies.

This cycle closes the loop—demonstrating that careerism is the core problem on generalship. Sure, some of our generals may (or may not) have been combat leaders as captains or lieutenant colonels, but once you pin a star on your shoulder, the political pressure mounts. Go-along-to-get-along, and get promoted, is the smoothest path. Don't rock the boat, do what your political masters tell you, never admit mistakes—and get promoted. Then, once you retire, you get to collect a pension and a sweet job from Lockheed Martin.

But, if you buck the system, you are not invited to the military-industrial complex cool-kids table. If you take accountability, you are shunned. If you question political leaders, you don't get promoted. If you speak out, you get passed over. If you reject woke, gender-neutral, race-based policies, you get fired—or probably never make one-star general anyway. Once any of that happens, you don't get the sweet gig with the defense industry.

Want to change this reality—and empower generals to be real leaders with the latitude to stand up for the Constitution? No general in the United States military should be allowed to work in the defense industry for ten years after they retire. That will help break the cycle.

Oh yeah, and fire any general who has carried water for Obama and Biden's extraconstitutional and agenda-driven transformation of our military. Clean house and start over.

Honor is what matters, not hitting bureaucratic milestones, achieving racial or gender "firsts," or accruing personal wealth. We need to return to reality, which means facing up to commonsensical truths.

The beginning of the end of the war on warriors starts here—don't miss this war either.

Chapter 4

THE LEFT'S *VERY SPECIAL* FORCES

The Left isn't just interested in purging Trump supporters. Their ideology is based on marginalizing whatever's normal, because they think "normal" is always oppressive. By their logic, the military runs on the most normal and most oppressive thing of all: strong men. Just being a guy who hits the gym means you're oppressing everyone around you, or something like that. That's why they're determined to fill the military with anything but that.

In wars and sports—where it's clear who wins and who loses—we value power, daring, and skill. The military has long been a place for turning boys into men by teaching those sorts of qualities. The Left sees all of them as oppressive, pointless, and irrelevant. Our enemies see them as they are: vital.

All of the following statements are simple realities, which means the Left finds them oppressive ideologies:

THE WAR ON WARRIORS

» Men are stronger than women.

» Men and women are different, with men being more aggressive.

» Men act differently toward women than they do other men.

» Men like women and are distracted by women. They also want to impress, and protect, women.

» Men who are pretending to be women, or vice versa, are a distraction. It might be your thing, but it's weird and does not add substantive value to anyone.

» Men respect other strong, skilled, dedicated men.

» Strong, skilled, dedicated men come in all shapes, sizes, and colors.

» Men don't give a shit what your skin color is, as long as you get the job done.

If you're being honest—and if you are not a politically correct lobotomy patient—you can't refute any of those statements. It's common sense. It's human nature. It's biology.

But today's military—thanks to Obama, Biden, and their lackeys—has rejected every statement I just made. They reject gender differences. They reject natural tendencies. They embrace "trans" lunacy. And they emphasize racial differences, instead of forging a shared identity. They have embraced gender identity and racial identity as ends to themselves, instead of small factors while otherwise forging the best possible team.

The Army I know, the Army we need, should be focused on outcomes. On forging individuals. On building teams. On shared missions. On winning battles. On winning wars. On outcomes. Anything that doesn't accomplish the mission is just a distraction. And, in war, distractions get people killed.

A man who has a feeling toward a female and acts differently in combat—gets people killed. A woman who can't do the same job as a man in combat—gets people killed. A "trans" soldier who doesn't have his/her meds is combat ineffective—and gets people killed. A competent, experienced white soldier who leaves the Army because he's been told he's the problem—gets people killed. Likewise, a black or female soldier who gets promoted, primarily because of the color of their skin or the genitalia between their legs—gets people killed.

The only thing that matters is mission accomplishment. Trained individuals. Trained teams. Shared missions. No distractions. Maximum lethality. Anything else is bullshit. And right now we have a steaming pile of it inside the Pentagon courtyard.

Step one of rejecting the framework of the Left is recognizing that we can't accept their language and assumptions. You are not oppressing anyone by existing. If you're in a minority, no one is oppressing you simply by existing. And the flip side of that is that no one should get an award just for checking a box.

June has always been an important month for the United States Army. The anniversary of D-Day is always a day of reverence. The Army's birthday is a week later in June. A large sheet cake would be cut by whatever officer had the cleanest cavalry sword—and often we did it live on *FOX & Friends*. June is always the month of four-day weekends and "training" holidays. That was until 2012, when the Obama/Biden administration reversed "Don't Ask, Don't Tell" and the military adopted the entire month of June as Pride Month.

Captain Nicole Wiswell is an engineer with the Minnesota National Guard. She (actually he) recently went viral with an Army-sponsored Pride Month video where the thirty-two-year-old stated, "as long as you show trust in your team and take care of your people, gender doesn't matter."

I guess the slogan "Gender Doesn't Matter" has a certain ring to it. When did the Army decide that this was forward-leaning messaging?

Perhaps one of the many reasons they are tens of thousands of soldiers—
men—short on the recruiting side.

When Major Rachel Jones cut an official video for the Army during
Pride Month, it doubled the traffic of any other Army pride month video
to date. Jones is the US Army Sustainment Command Cyber Division
Chief or G6 (Information Management). With his "she/her" pronouns
proudly displayed on the desk, Major Jones wants parents to know that
if they give their sons and daughters to defend the United States in
the Army, a major factor in the training will be reminding them that
"[d]iversity is our strength as a nation and what we (trans people) have to
offer in terms of diverse skill sets we bring, the diverse ways of thinking
we bring to the team to make everything work better."

If only Eisenhower had an out-of-shape transgender officer during
Operation Market Garden we could have ended World War II before
Christmas 1944.

As Major Jones goes on to explain on an Army-sponsored Twitter
video, he suffered major depression and had suicidal ideation before he
transitioned.

Jones said, "The pressure of hiding all the time was so bad I grew
up depressed and suicidal to the point that I always had a plan to end
my life. Even when deployed, the greatest threat to my own safety was
myself."

Well, I think we found the soldier of the quarter! But what PT standards will he use? By the look of him, he's a ten-push-up kind of guy.

You cannot maintain a security clearance in the military with suicidal ideation—let alone be the "chief" of a major Army cyber division.
Nor should you ever be trusted to oversee subordinates if you feel you are
a bigger threat to your own welfare than ISIS or Al Qaeda. No rational
soldier would ever say this aloud, let alone to the Army. I should be be-
fuddled that the Army vetted this video, edited it, and put their name

on it. But I'm not. Pride Month or not, this is a direct violation of every military standard there is. We have enough veteran suicide, yet here is a major in the United States Army talking about contemplating suicide while on deployment and now allegedly running a cyber shop with a full security clearance.

Complete insanity.

What has changed in the Army?

Well, Department of Defense Instruction 1300.28 is what changed in the Army. As of April 30, 2022, guidance was given for "In Service Transition for Transgender Service Members." When I served, "transition" meant you were leaving the military and took a class on how to do a job interview or how to fill out your VA paperwork. Now, under Secretary of Defense for Personnel and Readiness Virginia Penrod, the Pentagon has issued a step-by-step instruction book on what commanders and leaders *must* do to meet the needs of these very "special" forces.

In 2016, the Obama administration conducted a study to test whether it was a good idea after the repeal of "Don't Ask, Don't Tell" to allow transgender soldiers to openly serve in the military. That study found that post-surgery-transitioned soldiers would be nondeployable for 238 days or 34 weeks. When this report was brought to then–incoming president Donald Trump's attention, he promptly banned transgender soldiers from serving.

However, in 2022, Biden officials reversed the policy and issued 1300.28, which not only waived three hundred days for postop transgenders but also allowed for DoD hospitals to cover laser hair removal, voice feminization surgery, facial and body contouring procedures, breast/chest surgery, and genital surgery. They waived grooming standards and uniform standards for transgender soldiers as well. They then waived the standard that previously disqualified first-term elective surgery. This change to the standards meant that men and women could *join* the military for the express purpose of transitioning, be nondeployable for a year, and take life-altering hormone therapy that would mean they would be nondeployable unless the military could guarantee the supply of medication (you know, in some shithole country). Yes, your tax dollars pay for mentally unstable boys to become girls, chops off their body parts, then sit out of training for a year, pay for ongoing medical treatments, and demand everyone call them a new name. Man, I wish I had one of those supersoldiers in my platoon in Iraq.

I spoke with an "Alex Gordon" (pseudonym) who is an active-duty Army officer in the Field Artillery at Fort Hood, Texas. Graduating at the top of his class at West Point, he was commissioned in the past few years. "Gordon" got to experience the transgender shift in the Army in real time. Toward the end of his time at West Point, "lecture halls" became indoctrination seminars with social science professors giving mandatory beliefs. "White rage" was not just a catchphrase, it was the basis for study and briefings pushed by West Point professors. "When George Floyd was killed, we had a series of seminars where only black cadets were allowed to talk," Gordon told me.

The "woke" agenda was not just happening at West Point, but it followed this young officer to his duty station in Texas.

"Thursdays are leader time—I wanted to do training on radios. And skill-level stuff for our jobs. My boss called and said we needed to cancel training . . . for a transgender pronoun session. I mean, this happens all the time now."

Gordon's chain of command cannot question if someone in the unit wants to change their gender. He has soldiers in his unit enlisting under one sex, and then the DoD pays for them to immediately change to another gender. By the time they transition, their three-year enlistment is up and, because they are on "medical" and not available for training the entire time, they hardly served a day in the field artillery.

Look out, China!

"We have this one senior NCO [noncommissioned officer]. Old-school. The guy you want around to train young soldiers. Has seen and done everything. He called 'bullshit' on the bathrooms being all unisex. They forced him to apologize. When I do a briefing, I have to be super careful with pronouns—him, her, or whoever. Look, I'm junior officer, and it's really hard. I am literally walking on eggshells every day."

Gordon says in his unit overall readiness is in serious crisis. Enlisted at the ranks of E4 (Specialists) to E6 (Staff Sergeants) no longer want to reenlist. The "top block" (best) soldiers of his unit are getting out in droves. This leaves a junior NCO hole and forces units to promote soldiers not ready for that leadership position. If this is happening in one field artillery unit, what do you think is happening all over the Army? All over the military? As crazy as it sounds, the operational tempo during Iraq and Afghanistan made it better. At least the soldiers were busy, deploying and doing their jobs. Now they stand around in garrison getting lectured about their pronouns and unable to enforce basic standards.

Such pointless exercises are bound to generate resentment when the real-world lethality of the battlefield comes into play. "As far as I am concerned when it gets real, at war, you can't spell DIE without D-E-I. We need to do our jobs. This is life and death. I don't think these people understand or they simply don't care," Gordon told me. Soldiers must tell themselves, whenever lack of readiness in combat leads to terrible consequences: *at least we aren't misgendering our enemies!*

Even as Biden's military continued to market to the LGBTQIA+ (or whatever the acronym is by the time this is published) community, recruitment numbers plummeted, bordering on the realm of free fall. The military was self-evidently going "woke" and trying to appeal to nontraditional recruits to fill their quotas for the volunteer military.

The lack of deployment-ready units, because there are not enough new recruits, was one reason why the Pentagon resorted to a noncombat call-up of the Inactive Ready Reserve (IRR) for support in Europe in July 2023. The IRR, which I was a part of while writing this book, was not built to fill recruiting shortfalls of this magnitude. Biden's DoD is *desperate*.

Yet, instead of trying to avoid the looming recruiting iceberg, the military hit the accelerator and pushed their engines full steam ahead. More diversity! More gender worship! More trans celebration! Recruitment continued to fall *and* record numbers of enlisted soldiers decided to walk away from reenlistments, no matter how many perks the military was offering them. Huge bonuses . . . no thanks.

The administration and media will spin other reasons—like the economy or fitness levels of our youth—but the simple, underlying reason is clear: young people don't want to be a part of an organization that doesn't share their values. Even more, an organization they no longer trust. Or worst of all, an organization that doesn't trust, or want, *you*. How else do you explain a January 2024 revelation that Army recruiting numbers of white Americans have dropped precipitously in the past five years? From 44,000 white kids joining the Army in 2018, to 25,000 white kids joining in 2023—a staggering 43 percent decrease. At the same time, nonwhite demographics have seen increases those five years. Turns out, all the "diversity" recruiting messages made certain kids—white kids—feel like they're not wanted. It is a long-held conservative American tradition to speak softly . . . and walk away from organizations that offend our values. America's white sons and daughters are walking away, and who can blame them.

* * *

On April Fool's Day 2023, as part of a wildly stupid publicity campaign, Bud Light sent a package of special label cans to transgender influencer Dylan Mulvaney to commemorate his/her 365 days of "girlhood." The cans were intended to be part of a promotional sweepstakes that would give a potential winner $15,000 from Bud Light. Turns out the only *loser* was Bud Light.

Ten days later, Anheuser-Busch, the parent company of Bud Light, began to issue a steady stream of responses and quasi-retractions to navigate the resulting land mines to their own corporate image. Each resulting non-apology only made the problem worse. Who would have thought that Dylan Mulvaney, through "his" corporate deal with Bud Light, could create agreement between the patrons of Manhattan gay bars and Kid Rock? Somehow, all agreed they would boycott Bud Light, whose market share plummeted by $28 billion.

Anheuser-Busch was guilty of trying to find a new market by offending the values of their traditional customers. In their attempt to rebrand—and move beyond "frat boys," as one woke executive exclaimed—they lost their core customers, then offended those they were seeking to reach. Trying to please everyone caused them to lose everything.

The military says to Bud Light: hold by beer.

Joining the military is not a jobs program. It is a commitment, a passion, an act of sacrificial love. There is no draft. No one is forced to join. Those who join do so because they believe in the nation that they will be serving. Our recruits are intelligent, educated, morally upright, and good citizens. They are wise enough to know that they are giving themselves and their futures to the leadership of the United States of America.

Why then are so many turning their backs on a military career?

The military is paying the price for ignoring their core constituents for the sake of chasing social justice validation and nonexistent custom-ers. They are trading thousands of boys from Tennessee for a handful of trans recruits from San Francisco. People who join the military generally believe that joining provides a twofold benefit. It helps them become the people they want to become (it changes them for the better), and it does so in the service of a nation they respect (they become part of a noble tradition).

We have already mourned the lack of respect shown to the history and traditions of the nation and our military, so let's focus on military recruitment.

Military recruiters face a growing and persistent problem of the cur-rent generation: they want to be celebrated and praised for who they are, as if they arrive fully formed without the need for improvement and ma-turity. They desire to be accepted and acceptable as they see themselves, with the impetus placed on others to accept their condition, assump-tions, and worldview without question.

Soldiers are traditionally offered none of these incentives. They en-ter the military unformed; they are broken, shaped, and molded into the soldiers that they can become. They are trained to fit into the mold that the military has prepared for them, not to be themselves to the cheers of the brass. They are pushed to always be better, to never settle on being good enough, to never anticipate or expect praise, and to do the difficult work when no one is watching them. Spotlight Rangers (attention hogs) and individualists are not good recruits and will be winnowed away by boot camp and rigorous training exercises. Seeking them in recruitment drives is not only foolish but counterproductive to the maintenance of a strong military.

* * *

In this book, I have said consistently that our military needs people who will protect and defend the Constitution of the United States and are willing to fight, bleed, and kill in its defense. You may ask, if that is the goal, then why not have transgenders in the military? The answers are physical, biological, and medical.

There are multiple controversial debates surrounding transgenderism in the Western world. One debate surrounds the coeducational imposition of transgenders in athletics, locker rooms, and school restrooms. This debate concerns the unwanted exposure to/of naked bodies in public/private spaces and is grounded in the clash of "rights" between the trans person and the women who must coexist in these traditionally safe spaces. This has to do with a right to safety and privacy in intimate moments.

Another controversy regards underaged trans children and body-altering procedures, therapies, and surgeries. The transition of a minor child involves issues of consent and maturity. Do children under eighteen fully understand the decision that they are making? Is there a compelling reason for a society that bans those under twenty-one from alcohol and those under eighteen from nicotine and tattoos to abandon these commonsense restrictions for procedures that are far more life-changing and permanent? It's an insane and illogical double standard pushed by the godless Left in pursuit of altering the male-female construct.

While all of these might be controversial, they rate an open debate in a free society. But they only tangentially impact our discussion of transgenders in the military because such concerns must be applied against the standard of *combat readiness and efficacy.*

When it comes to transgenderism in the military, the shuttering of the "Don't Ask, Don't Tell" policies during the Obama administration effectively created a dual reality: soldiers can do what they want sexually in their own time *and* a soldier's sexual life is now open at work.

Homosexuality was no longer disqualifying for a military cadet or enlisted person, so the moral and/or cultural rationale for barring transgenders collapsed.

The concern with transgenderism in the military is not about the individual rights of the person or the collective rights of the unit. The concerns are based on the standards of military readiness and the likely failure of a transitioning and/or transitioned person to meet those standards.

To understand why military readiness is impacted by transgenderism and transitioning, you just have to look at what the expectations of a soldier are. When a Marine or soldier goes to basic training the first thing they will notice, especially if they are an allergy sufferer, is that they are not allowed to use their allergy medications without authorization from the medic. For many of them in the opening days of the hot, humid, and sweltering boot camp, the lack of their normal allergy medications results in significant headaches.

One might ask the question, why does boot camp restrict the soldier from using their allergy medications? Well, the same reason boot camp makes sure that the Soldiers, Sailors, and Marines are given military-issued glasses instead of their custom civilian eyewear. The recruit is not training for the local field hockey team, or the Google soccer squad. They are being prepared for war. Military readiness means preparing the soldier for the depravations of the combat situation. Civilian eyewear typically is not capable of withstanding the rigors of battle, nor does it easily work with the gear that the soldier must wear in the combat zones. It is not about your personal comfort or your appearance; it is about your effectiveness in the field that matters.

It's the same with allergy meds. The military cannot guarantee that you will have your medication when you're on field assignment. Nor can they assume that your brand of nasal spray will not interact with the jabs, meds, and toxins that you will be exposed to in a combat zone. The goal is to minimize the risks and needs of the combat troops in the field. The more they are dependent upon, the less combat ready they become. If you are fighting for days at a time, or in a submarine or on a flight deck, the issue must become, can you endure it if you lose access to the medications that you need?

Before deploying to combat, I very much remember the dental exams. Seemed odd at the time. But makes sense now. There was a category level for dentistry that deployed soldiers must meet. A category four or "CAT 4" was someone who needed surgery, a root canal, or filling. If those procedures were not completed by a certain day, the tooth was simply pulled. That was the only way you would end up deploying with your unit. Why? The Army did not want a toothache in the desert, where dentists were in short supply. Any issue had to be removed for the betterment of the mission. I deployed with many soldiers who just had teeth pulled, usually with not enough anesthesia. The mission always comes first.

One of the realities of a transgender person is that they are dependent on medications and hormones to live as the gender that they have chosen. They are nondeployable for almost a year after transition. It is not as simple as having surgery and going on with your life. Transgender people must maintain a regular regime of medication, or their hormones will reregulate to the natural/birth standards. It takes a lot of medication to manage self-mutilation.

No team should want someone who puts themselves above the organization. You do not want someone already burdened by the rigors and stress of a combat situation that also may be experiencing a hormonal shift. Our hormones regulate our emotions and have a link to our behaviors. You can't be in a combat situation and be forced to address the lack of medication that changes your behavior, attitudes, or capabilities in the field. More importantly, your fellow soldiers shouldn't have to deal with it.

When bullets fly, and they will, that's what matters.

Another Army senior NCO weighed in for me: "Every time we get our biannual extremism training, or transgender in your formation training, I don't know a single person who doesn't roll their eyes and say 'what the fuck are we doing.'"

We all roll our eyes . . . but the policy continues, and it consumes the unit.

To be blunt, the *real* military doesn't care about your pronouns, or any other customized communication concerns you may have. Your squad and company couldn't care less about these things. The offenses that our combat soldiers experience every day on the battlefield are the true and critical test of human endurance.

As each Soldier, Sailor, and Marine is put through the test of boot camp, many are demeaned and criticized by drill sergeants to toughen them up and prepare them for things that are much more damaging to the body, mind, and spirit. If a soldier falls apart because they are called by the wrong pronoun, then they are not mentally strong enough to endure the rigors of combat. If they are not, then they have no business being in a combat-ready military force.

You cannot care about an individual when the collective—the interlocking parts of a smooth, steady, yet complex military machine—is in the balance. Let me be abundantly clear. Like my old platoon sergeant used to say to our guys, "Sorry if Mom and Dad never told you this at home . . ." For the most part, the Army, the Air Force, the Marines, the Navy, and the Coast Guard have no issue with what guys legally do on their own time, within the guidelines of the chain of command. When it encroaches upon the function and mission of the unit, it cannot be allowed. It must be removed for the betterment of the team.

Americans have been trained to believe that our sexual choices are private and unassailable. This, of course, is a relatively recent innovation, but one that I am not averse to acknowledging (mostly). What you wish to do in the privacy of your own home and on your own time is yours. But once you have freely joined the United States military, you have surrendered your time, your body, and your privacy. It's not about *you*, it's about *us*.

You are no longer your own person. The lives of your brothers are in your hands. The sake of our nation hangs in the balance.

You are a part of the most disciplined and lethal force in human history. That was why you sport the bad haircut. That's why you must wear a uniform. That's why you aren't allowed to have facial hair like you did during your summer abroad. That's why you wear the uncomfortable boots. That is why you might miss the birth of your son, or the wedding of your sister. That is why the patch on your shoulder is the flag of the United States of America. The same flag that stands for American pride—not gay or trans pride.

The military does not care if you look better in fall colors, because you surrender your individuality to be a part of an organization that must stand for something bigger than any one person or ideology. In the military we are not white or brown, we are not Methodists or Mormons, we are not homosexual or heterosexual, we are just Americans. Dedicated, disciplined, lethal Americans. Anything that distracts from the objectives of mission success must be surrendered for the sake of the nation.

The rules and conditions of the military were established well before our grandparents joined. Wisdom of wars past forged our combat standards. Our responsibility, like theirs, is to comply—and have courage. Small improvements are made. Equipment improves. But the oath never does. All of this might seem "mean" to those who have lived civilian lives with civilian privileges. If you lose an arm at the plant, you will sue the company and likely win big. If you lose a limb in the Army, it is a part of your service. Talk to someone who's lost a limb for the country. Talk to someone who's lost a brother or sister in battle.

If you are *not* willing to lay down your life, or a limb, for the sake of a bigger cause, then you really should look at another career. If you want to dress in drag and be "affirmed," then move to San Francisco. But our American military has no business falsely advertising anything that is contrary to its warfighting ethos, regardless of their recruitment goals or political expectations.

For the recruits, for the military, and primarily for the security of the country, transgender people should never be allowed to serve. It's that simple.

Chapter 5

THE (DEADLY) OBSESSION WITH WOMEN WARRIORS

It was the biggest movie of 2022. Steven Spielberg gushed that it "saved Hollywood's ass" after COVID restrictions had driven Americans to stay home and stream old favorites. He probably thought its success was based on simple nostalgia. But what was it about *Top Gun: Maverick* that sent people streaming back to theaters?

I'll give you a hint: It wasn't just spectacle. It was something deeper. It was the fact that this was a story about how America, Americans, brave men, normal men, and heroism were all *good* things. It was a breath of fresh air.

In the sequel to the original feel-good American hype movie, Tom Cruise's ace pilot Maverick Mitchell starts off as the embodiment of modern American ennui. Paralyzed by guilt over past mistakes, he's stalled in his career, refusing to be the leader the military needs. What if he makes a mistake and gets someone else hurt?

When a crisis comes along, he drags his feet, unwilling to step up to take responsibility.

Ultimately, he is forced to learn that he needs to stop overprotecting his soldiers—a good dad doesn't swaddle his kids in bubble wrap or keep them on the bench. He empowers them, lets them go hard on their own, and promises to always have their back. That spirit of risk and honor is the *only* thing that can neutralize the threat.

The movie is a giant depiction of a hero arguing with a safety-obsessed careerist bureaucracy to get a tough job done in a way that won't needlessly sacrifice the young people in his command.

Can you imagine the stream of new recruits our military would see if that was our ethos, front and center?

The Army has a safety problem, which is only getting worse. It's not that today's wokesters created an obsession with safety, but they have exacerbated it. By definition, what the military does is *not* safe. Kill or be killed. Destroy or be destroyed. Not exactly safe. Understandably, the military—over the years—has worked hard to make training safer to minimize casualties and injuries. And, despite highly publicized recent training accidents, the military overall does a pretty good job keeping troops safe when they train.

But if you talk to guys still serving—and I talked to many for this book—they will point out that a big reason for fewer training accidents is . . . less training. More time than ever is being spent on social justice PowerPoint moralizing—and meeting those metrics in today's military is the most important standard to meet. One former Army battalion commander told me, "The Army doesn't give a shit about training anymore. Instead, how long can Private Snuffy grow his beard before we can kick him out?" A Marine Corps enlisted veteran told me, "In our force, it is impossible to do all the nonsense training . . . and also maintain our gunnery standards. Or vehicle maintenance training. You are naturally going to have to sacrifice training to do your political reeducation bullshit. There is only a finite amount of time."

Another colonel still heavily involved in unit training said "the Army 'trans' PowerPoint training sucks. If you try to get into a conversation, they shut you down. I had two NCOs that were disgusted by the training. I tell them how I feel candidly, but nothing changes. There are three people in a command of one thousand who identify as 'trans'—and we do the daylong training every six months for point three percent of our unit." Another midlevel Army officer told me after conducting this very training himself—for weeks on end—"I was getting phone calls from senior officer saying, 'I'm tracking these ten dudes didn't do the brief. Get it done!' My senior officers were all over me like hawks on the trans shit—in ways they never do for real warfighting tasks. It all just means we keep people in the classroom longer than we need to, and real training just gets delayed. Or never happens."

These are just a few direct quotes. And I could go on and on. Unit by unit. Day by day. It's not just junior enlisted, or senior enlisted. Junior officers or senior officers. It's across the military, and it has become an obsession. Every unit knows that social justice, trans, gender, woke training is the top priority. Not doing this training, or not doing it properly, will get a commander or junior leader fired. Not doing real field training becomes secondary. They say it is to make people feel "safe," but everybody knows—even the people mandating this training—that when the bullets start flying, this approach is going to make everybody less safe.

Ultimately, this type of approach is not the fault of the troops—it is the fault of the general class. Much like the brass that show up in *Top Gun: Maverick*, today's highest-ranking military leaders are simultaneously negligent about protecting soldiers on the battlefield and absurdly safety-conscious in training, a small-minded approach that erodes readiness in the long run. They have bought into this feedback loop, so military leaders focus on becoming efficient bureaucrats, not honorable warriors.

Which takes us back to the problem of careerism. The generals, serving under Obama and now Biden, know that far left-wing social justice crap is coming down the pike. It's their job to stand up to it, resign, or, as most of them have done, just give in to it. Going along gets these generals along—and their careers continue. And then, when they retire, they get to sit at the defense contractor cool-kids table. All the colonels I know who were real warfighters—who would never cave to this stuff—have long since been pushed out of the military. The social-justice safety-obsessed keep getting promoted.

Which, again, makes all the troops less safe. Safety is not what built America. Grit built America. Toughness built America. Taking risks built America. And, right now, our military leadership does not embody any of those things. America sent men to the moon in a spaceship that had a fraction of the technology of my iPhone. Where are such men today? They are not wearing camouflage with stars on their shoulder, that's for sure.

I'm going to say something politically incorrect but that is a perfectly commonsensical observation: Dads push us to take risks. Moms put the training wheels on our bikes. We need moms. *But not in the military, especially in combat units.*

It's not that individual women can't be courageous, ambitious, and honorable. I know many phenomenal female soldiers. The problem is that the Left needs *every* woman to be as successful as every man, so they've redefined success in a counterproductive way. The Left doesn't praise the exceptional women who demonstrate martial qualities, but rather redefines the goals we need in the military to be more conducive to female success. The problem is that a more empathetic and effeminate military isn't a more efficient one. It's a more *inefficient* one. That puts everyone at risk. Which, again, is a really bad thing in the business of killing.

The gender integration of the military is a huge part of our modern confusion about the goals of war. In particular, the choice to put women in combat roles. The Left is at war with the reality of differences between men and women, and the Right, in a misguided effort to be chivalrous and inclusive, has forgotten basic truths about reality. Conservatives have caved in the face of self-evident realities about the limitations women face in combat. Common sense, out the window.

* * *

Consider women in combat and the way it's completely common in modern stories, whereas it was quite rare in old ones. The old comic book version of "super women" at war was a generational distillation of women in combat. Unlike the mythologies of great Amazonian warriors in the Greek mythologies, most of the world's accounts of women at war were connected to seductive and sexual power. Instead of Wonder Woman, much of Western poetry and stories focuses on four types of warrior women: the seductress, the supplanter (substitute), the sacrifice, and the saint.

There was the seductress, typified by Cleopatra, the Macedonian queen of Ptolemaic Egypt who seduced both Julius Caesar and his protégé Mark Antony. Biblical women like Esther, who used beauty and hospitality to charm her husband, the king of Persia, in order to save her Jewish brethren. Jael, in the Bible's book of Judges, chapter 4, pacifies, tricks, and executes the invading General Sisera, using not sexual power but cunning hospitality.

The imagery from Judges, chapter 5, shows a woman using domestic weapons to persuade the enemy leader, Sisera, to let down his guard and fall asleep in her tent. Sisera enters Jael's domestic space but is ultimately defeated when she breaks this maternal intimacy by turning a masculine weapon against him.

> [24] *Most blessed of women be Jael,*
> *the wife of Heber the Kenite,*
> *most blessed of tent-dwelling women.*
> [25] *He asked for water, and she gave him milk;*
> *in a bowl fit for nobles she brought him curdled milk.*
> [26] *Her hand reached for the tent peg,*
> *her right hand for the workman's hammer.*
> *She struck Sisera, she crushed his head,*
> *she shattered and pierced his temple.*
> [27] *At her feet he sank,*
> *he fell; there he lay.*
> *At her feet he sank, he fell;*
> *where he sank, there he fell—dead.*

While Stan Lee was more than comfortable portraying superwomen with the power of invisibility, and in the classic role of the black widow seductress, it wasn't until the middle of the 1970s that the superwomen took on a more aggressive and traditionally masculine role in the comics.

Another historical role for women in combat has echoed through history: that of the abandoned woman, who was left without a protector and who must rise to the occasion. This is the role of the supplanter or substitute, the one who takes the place of someone incapable or unwilling to fight. In the Old Testament this is the story of Deborah, who leads the Jewish people when the general that God calls refuses to act alone.

While Barak leads the army, Deborah receives the credit as Barak will not take responsibility for the battle. Historically this was evidenced in women leading because there was no man to lead—women that rise to the throne in the absence of a suitable male heir. Many of these powerful women are well known to history, Queen Elizabeth I of England and Queen Catherine the Great of Russia being two of the most notable. Important for our topic, it should be noted that supplanters rarely take an actual role in battle.

Some, however, especially in the "barbarian" cultures of the Western world and in Viking history, take the reins as leaders in battle, usually due to the dramatic deaths of their fathers or husbands or the need for "shield maidens"—or archers in circumstances in which combat troops are in short supply. Things rarely work out for them. They are most renowned as sacrificial soldiers, leading a pyrrhic charge against odds that provide little hope for true victory. Some of the more famous combat warriors include women like Queen Boudicca, who was known as a barbarian queen who led an AD 60 counterrevolution against Roman troops in England as the de facto leader of the Iceni, a Celtic tribe. While Queen Boudicca found initial victories with guerrilla attacks in pre–Anglo-Saxon London, she was eventually destroyed by a small group of radically outnumbered Roman soldiers.

Perhaps the most famous Western woman warrior was the French saint Joan of Arc—a sacrificial saint. Joan's story was once again a story like the biblical Deborah, her rise to power in the fading days of the Hundred Years War, when the French grew tired of the endless fighting with England. She brought a message of monarchial success to King Charles VII of France and buttressed the French resistance to English invasion at the siege of Orleans. While her actions certainly brought favor to Charles and increased the morale of the French military, her battlefield prowess was not as advertised. She was soon captured on the battlefield and sent to the English, who tried her as a heretic and burned her at the stake at the age of nineteen.

While many of these ancient warriors and queens captivate modern imaginations, almost all of them are victims of broken kingdoms and could boast only of pyrrhic victories. They are predominantly daughters of kings and historically represent the last embers of decaying dynasties usurped by more powerful empires who swept their peoples from the pages of history.

It should also be noted that the lion's share of these legends spoke not to the efficacy of women in combat roles, but more importantly to the efficacy of their gods. The overwhelming narratives of women in combat in the ancient world are stories that reflect a bias that the "gods" of the people are so powerful and righteous that even a child, a female child, like Joan of Arc can be used to defeat the British military. Deborah was not a mighty warrior; she was a faithful follower of the mighty warrior God of Israel.

There are examples in history of women in combat roles, but one is hard-pressed to find many, outside of religious or mythological settings, that have anything close to a positive military outcome.

This is the "macro" reason why Western nations have resisted women in direct combat roles. Not only are women comparatively less effective than men in combat roles, but they are also more likely to be objectified by the enemy and their own nation in the moral realms of war.

* * *

In the modern world the nations that utilize women in combat the most are usually totalitarian nations (save for Israel); often children and teenagers are also freely utilized in combat situations. It is hard to congratulate the progressive instinct of the North Koreans, the Viet

Cong, the Nazis, the Ugandans, or the Soviets, when these nations were also throwing adolescent boys into combat roles due to a lack of available fighting men. Around the world women are usually used in combat roles by tyrants and war lords; the same war lords who use child soldiers.

At first, United States military leaders decided that the best place for women in the armed forces was in a support role. Women bring life into the world. Their role in war is to make it a less deathly experience. The United States followed the Western Christian tradition that women were best suited to carry the banner of Christian love into the darkest moments of warfare and devastation. For this reason, women became the sainted care givers of the Red Cross, typified in Clara Barton. Barton left her city hospital to give aid to Civil War soldiers in the field. In the Battle of Antietam, she helped render aid to almost ten thousand wounded Union soldiers in three Army wagons. She was a logistical powerhouse.

Wherever the United States military fought there were women in combat zones. They carried the banner of safety, peace, and care. They were mothers, sisters, and angels of combat. In the mythologies of the United States military, as well as in their ad campaigns, women represented all that was good and pure in the world. Of course, this was not always factually true, but all mythologies are attempts at creating order out of the chaos of the world. While Joan of Arc was a French saint due to her tepid history of military success, President Trump would be correct to call her a "loser" for her final three battles that ended disastrously and eventually with her execution.

The truth is that the women who served in noncombat roles in field hospitals and resource centers experienced many of the traumas of combat for themselves. Many a chaplain and field doctor suffer from PTSD. In the finale of the famous TV series *M*A*S*H*, Korean War surgeon

"Hawkeye" Pierce is being treated for shell shock (or PTSD) without ever carrying a weapon or lining up in a trench. American and Western women have suffered and sacrificed for the sake of others for generations. To ignore their sacrifice, or minimize it, ignores the intricate web of work that is necessary to maintain the military at war. As Russia's adventure in Ukraine has taught us all in high definition, wars are won and lost on severed supply lines or lost communications. Intelligence gathering, chow lines, equipment maintenance, fuel, and medical support are all an essential part of the war effort. They are the difference between bitter defeat and victory. Women have nobly assisted the war effort in dangerous support roles for generations. We know they can do this, but the issue surrounding women in the infantry—women in combat on purpose—is another story.

The gender integration of these traditionally male spheres, coupled with our loss of a Christian ethos for God's creation, means we've started to think of men and women as essentially the same animal with different levels of body strength. That's particularly dangerous when it comes to combat because the differences aren't just physical. The American issue with women in combat was always functionally twofold.

First, do we want women to become killers?

The Spartans had one of the most militaristic civilizations in history, yet they did not utilize women in combat roles. Their reasoning was quite simple: they needed the women to act as mothers to train up the men who would populate the Spartan army. The toughest men learned how to sacrifice from watching the sacrificial work of their mothers. Women are life givers, regardless of what the abortion industry might want us to think. This role was embedded in human beings and was one of the clear reasons why the only, even mythologically articulated, successful women in combat narratives involve separatist societies of non-childbearing women who live apart from men. To create a society of warrior women you must separate them first from men, and then from the natural purposes of their core instincts.

Second, how do we want men to treat women, both in our military and among the enemy?

The second core question regarding the impact of women in the infantry and in combat roles is societal. How do you treat women in a combat situation without eroding the basic instinct of civilization and the treatment of women in the society at large?

How are men supposed to treat women in combat zones? The military acronym is COBS, Civilians on the Battlespace. The Hague routinely uses the terms "women and children" purposively to evoke the barbarity of violations of the laws of land warfare. One of the most difficult aspects of armed combat are the situations that soldiers experience when they must suppress their natural instincts, for the sake of the greater mission.

In a civilized society you cannot steal your neighbor's car without being seen as a criminal. In a civilized society we are trained to treat women differently than we treat men. If a boy punches a girl in civilized society, that has always been considered brutality. That's not just because of social norms, but also because the average man's upper-body strength is greater than that of 99 percent of women.

When a young man punches his fiancée in a hotel elevator, we not only condemn the behavior, but he finds himself ostracized, and loses his NFL contract and endorsement deals. No one argued that his behavior was anything but horrific and no one defended him as "triggered" by her behaviors. She didn't "deserve it." His behavior was anathematized not because he hit someone, but because he hit a woman.

Women in combat forces men to ignore those civilized instincts. If you train a group of men to treat women equally on the battlefield then you will be hard-pressed to ask them to treat women differently at home. Which leads to the vexing cliché that has plagued every warrior since Vietnam:

» Veterans are damaged.
» Veterans are dangerous.
» Veterans do not matriculate normally into society after war.

What about women combat veterans? What does that look like? We have no idea.

So, you can imagine how shocking it was to the military when, in 2015, the Obama administration started integrating combat jobs (known as "military occupational specialties") with women. Most branches, led by feckless military leaders, bent their needs to the political winds and quickly brushed off the realities of human nature, biological sex differences, and combat reality. Again, cowardly generals caving to beta-male politicians.

The military talked a good game, but it was a sham. "The department's policy is that all ground combat positions will be open to women unless rigorous analysis of factual data shows that the positions must remain closed," said Secretary of Defense Ash Carter in 2015.

About that factual data . . .

In 1992, the George H. W. Bush administration did a presidential commission on military combat effectiveness post–Gulf War. The study found that a "military unit is less likely to suffer casualties when at maximum combat effectiveness." Simply put, trained, steady, and violent equals more lethal. More lethal equals more veterans marching on Main Street for the Veterans Day parade back home—instead of being remembered at the Memorial Day parade.

In 2015—following the Obama administration's demand for "factual data"—the United States Marine Corps released a study on women fighting alongside men. The Ground Combat Element Integrated Task Force (ITF) was made up of 300 male Marines and 100 female Marines who trained together at Twenty-Nine Palms in California and were compared to a group of 400 all-male Marines. The ITF was comprised of 134 tasks performed that would determine a training environment akin to battle-like conditions. A study was compiled, and one thousand pages showed us what any sane person who spent two days in a field exercise or doing PT since *forever* would state: the all-male units blew away the gender-integrated unit. (Remember, this was not a fifty-fifty comparison—even the male-female unit was overwhelmingly male. Otherwise, results would have been more dramatic.)

The all-male Marines performed better 70 percent of the time—completing 93 out of the 134 tasks better than the gender-integrated units. The all-male Marines were found to be faster and more accurate with weapons. Which, you know, is pretty damn important when you are in the business of killing the enemy.

The gender-integrated did lead the all-male Marines in one important category: *injuries.*

Yes, the female Marines were injured at twice the rate of the men:

> *The Marines found that women in the integrated unit were injured twice as often, less accurate with infantry weapons and not as good at removing wounded comrades from the line of fire. Units comprising all men also were faster than units with women at completing tactical movements, especially while carrying large "crew-served" weapons like machine guns and mortars, the study found.*
> —Washington Post, *October 15, 2015*

Then–secretary of the Navy Ray Mabus told NPR in 2015, "part of the study said that we're afraid that because women get injured more frequently, that over time women will break down more—that you will begin to lose your combat effectiveness over time. That was not shown in this study. That was an extrapolation based on injury rates, and I'm not sure that's right."

Brilliant analysis, Ray. Spoken like a dutiful Obama appointee, drawing from his two years of noncombat time in the Navy. What a fucking idiot, but a useful one. A useful idiot okay with lying in a way that will get future American daughters injured . . . and killed. So-called men like Ray Mabus, whose name is long forgotten, is typical of the self-interested and stealth saboteurs behind the war on warriors.

His logic: just because *our* female Marines broke down when training with all-male Marines, that doesn't mean that *all* female Marines will break down when fighting with male Marines.

They must have just gotten some defective female Marines. Just because 39 percent of Americans in the Gallup poll disapproved of the Biden administration doesn't mean that 39 percent of all Americans disapprove of the Biden administration.

The numbers, the studies, and plain realities would not deter dutiful left-wing ideologues.

What then is the point of the study if not an extrapolation of the entire branch? Polls and studies are extrapolations. That's why they are called studies. Otherwise, you might as well make the "study" a real-world deployment where scores of infantry Marines lose their life so Ray can humble brag about his gender-diverse Marine Corps.

The media didn't know how to report on this study in 2015, so they did what they always do: they talked out of both sides of their mouths . . . and out their asses.

While all-male units significantly outperformed integrated ones, integrated groups excelled at complex decision-making. The report found that adding women to the unit also improved the behavior of the group as a whole.

"Integration of females is likely to lower the instance of disciplinary action, and this has been shown in general across the Marine Corps," the report said.

But the document also found that seven sexual assaults were reported by members of the unit, though the study noted that Marines in the ITF reported sexual assault "at levels similar to those in other military populations'" (ABC News, October 16, 2015).

So, the discipline was *better* while serving with female Marines, but there were seven allegations of sexual assault. Wait, what? And according to these sources at ABC News, "nothing to see here." That is what normally happens when units train for war? After only four months of range time? Did this training occur at Tailhook or Twenty-Nine Palms?

In fiscal year 2014, there were 6,131 reports of sexual assault in the DoD made against a cohort of approximately 1,354,054 service members in uniform during that same year. These reports are of allegations that are investigated and they are not proven assaults until they are adjudicated. The percentage of total service members who served versus alleged sexual assaults is 0.45 percent. Those are male and female sexual assaults combined. In that exercise in Twenty-Nine Palms it was alleged that 2.33 percent of the female Marines were sexually assaulted.

It's not a perfect apples-to-apples comparison, but that's a pretty big difference. The Marine Corps stated that the assaults were not "during" the training but occurred in the time frame of the training. Somehow, that will not impact morale? It was all an excuse, meant to spin away from the main point: this was a monstrously bad report for the Obama administration—on and off the battlefield—and a huge distraction to the proud United States Marine Corps.

Alleged assaults aside, the women struggled. And in war, struggling at physical competence leads to people getting hurt. People getting hurt means less rounds downrange. Depleted morale. And death. Defeat and carnage.

All-male units were faster in moving to a target, the study found, especially with a heavy weapon like a machine gun. They also had more hits on target and at a faster rate. And the number of females in those mixed-gender units was small. They tested with one woman, then two women. The numbers were kept low to reflect this reality. Women make up just 7 percent of the Marine Corps.

The study pointed to what it called notable differences in the amount of time it took an all-male unit to evacuate a wounded Marine compared to a mix-gender unit. In addition, women had trouble climbing over a barrier with their packs and often needed assistance. And they suffered more injuries, like stress fractures from carrying heavy packs. Still, the Marines included no specific time differences in the synopsis, and they said the findings do not necessarily mean that women should be barred from ground combat.

—NPR, September 10, 2015

There was always some lame "elitist" defense for the performance of the woman. The study could have found that female Marines over-packed for the field problem and took too long to decide what MRE to eat. Or that they gossiped more, or less. None of it mattered. Simply put, the agenda was more important than the readiness of our combat units during a war.

And, finally, the Left ignored their holy grail: the science. Men have greater bone density, men have more muscle mass, and men have more lung capacity. Men are, gasp, biologically stronger, faster, and bigger.

Dare I say, physically *superior*. These are established scientific facts, all of which were completely ignored by the "party of science."

Add all this together—the studies and the science—and it should be devastating to the White House. This was a horrible performance. And according to Secretary of Defense Ash Carter and his search for "factual data," this would mean that they would pause the integration of females into ground combat units.

Of course not. The ideology must prevail.

* * *

Because the Left is determined to make their gender-neutral future a reality, they've redefined the goals of success in the military.

They don't care how many battles we lose as long as our dead are diverse. We can see this in how the woke PR machine has spun stories of female service.

In the post-9/11 wars, there are three female names that history remembers. First, Jessica Lynch. The specialist who was taken hostage. The victim. Horrible things happened to her, and she was still (contrary to her wishes) turned into a hero by the military PR machine, looking for a "first." Her unit did not fire a round at the enemy and their convoy got lost and drove into the awaiting enemy. Think Custer's Last Stand if Custer asked Sitting Bull for directions at Little Bighorn.

Second, Lynndie England. She was an enlisted soldier out of the 372nd Military Police Army Reservist unit out of Maryland. She was famous for torturing naked Iraqi prisoners at Abu Ghraib Prison in Baghdad. One could argue that the behavior of this one unit at Abu Ghraib led to more Americans killed in action than any one event in the Iraq War.

Lynndie could have been sentenced to eleven years if her first trial hadn't ended in a mistrial. Her noncommissioned officer was to blame. She pleaded to three years and served seventeen months. To boot, Lynndie was impregnated by another soldier in her unit. While they couldn't defend her behavior, some liberals still stretched to paint her as a victim of her superiors, even though Lynndie continued to defend her abhorrent actions as ultimately good. Lynndie was a strong and powerful individual, right up until she committed war crimes, it turns out. Meanwhile, liberals complain about the Geneva Conventions and the policy that led us to war in Iraq, somehow excusing away the decision-making process of the worst military police unit in the American military. I can't remember off the top of my head what Army regulation states that you can't do drugs, drink alcohol, and impregnate your lower enlisted soldier on a combat deployment, but I'm pretty sure it's in there.

And Brigadier General Janis Karpinski, who was in charge of Abu Ghraib? She wrote a book. She did numerous appearances on MSNBC. She got demoted to colonel not for Abu Ghraib abuses, but for "dereliction of duty." May I remind you: this is a stout and squared-away unit.

Ain't no party like 372nd Military Police Party, cause the 372nd don't stop!

The two most famous females in the so-called War on Terror were a victim and a criminal.

Until we get to number three—Leigh Ann Hester, an NCO with the Kentucky National Guard's 617th Military Police Company. In March 2005, her convoy was attacked by thirty Anti-Iraqi Forces (AIF was the dystopian acronym we used in Iraq). SSG Hester got out of her Humvee and assaulted the enemy with her squad leader. She killed three AIF forces by herself. She shot a 40mm grenade, threw two frags, and fired her M4. Hester was the first female in the military since World War II to be awarded the Silver Star.

I like Leigh Ann Hester. She is an incredible soldier and did her job when it counted.

Are there more Leigh Ann Hesters on the ground, shooting bad guys in our military today? What about in the last twenty years? I think we certainly would have heard about they/them by now.

The assumptions of those seeking to sexually integrate our combat units wrongly conclude that adding women to the combat ranks will have the same social impact as racial integration did in the 1950s.

They are wrong. *So* wrong.

While racial integration of the military went a long way to proving to white men that black men were owed respect and appreciation, this does not mean that integrating women into the military will have the same impact. The first issue was that black men earned the respect due to them for the work that they were able to accomplish. Think about it like a sports team. If you are integrating a Spanish-speaking team with an English-speaking team, what binds them together is the ability to play the game they love. Team sports teams can bridge the language barrier because of their common understanding of the game. They will work together to make the team better, but they will not grow to appreciate each other unless they actually begin to win. If the English speakers can't play the game, the Spanish speakers will begin to resent them and fracture the chemistry of the team.

Any social tinkering with a team has the potential to destroy chemistry, especially when the goal of the team is to win. In combat this is exponentially more important. The reason that racial integration worked in the military was that black men and white men have equal capabilities on the battlefield and in the crucible of training. Integration proves equality when equality is evidenced: it *undermines* equality when the evidence of equality is not proven on the battlefield and in the crucible of training.

This means the only way to allow for women in combat that maintains combat readiness is for the standards of men and women to be the same. If a sniper needs to have a particular effectiveness, then there can be only one standard and that must be based on the effective standard, not a manufactured one created to show inclusion. To put it bluntly, NFL fans, owners, or teammates would not object to a female field goal kicker who could consistently hit a 60-yard field goal under pressure, but team chemistry would collapse if she only had 40-yard range, missed her first five kicks, the team was losing . . . and she remained on the team. Teams are fused not only by common training, but on common capabilities. Trust might not be easily offered, but it can be earned by merit and effectiveness. If women are not held to the same standard as men in combat units, then their inclusion will create animosity and anger in the ranks.

Seems simple, right? Well, simple is really hard for angry liberals.

The problem is that the goal isn't to make the best and deadliest group of soldiers, but to make sure that people aren't engaging in wrongthink about women's potential. Secretary of the Navy Ray Mabus in 2015 told NPR, "It started out with a fairly large component of the men thinking this is not a good idea and women will never be able to do this. When you start out with that mindset, you're almost presupposing the outcome." Maybe the power of positive thinking will increase women's muscle mass!

(By the way, the reason we talk about loser Ray Mabus so much is that his betrayal of the Marine Corps was so stark. The other services just caved to the edicts of the Obama administration. The leadership of the Army and Air Force surrendered without a fight. The Marine Corps at least fought back, but was undercut by a weak, political, and lying secretary of the Navy.)

Physical limitations are real. Unless of course you think you can jump off the Pentagon and fly safely down to the bottom. Even if all your friends tell you it is a bad idea, but you charge forward and jump scream-ing, "Ray Mabus is correct!" you are still landing on your head. Your friends who first told you it was a very bad idea are not bigoted or narrow-minded—they are correct. Even though all available data from the field show that sexual integration of combat units is a bad idea, the leaders don't care. They like studies only when they reinforce their stupidity.

So, since women cannot physically meet the same standards as men, the military has two options—both bad. They can lower the standards for everyone to ensure more women meet with infantry or combat stan-dards. Or they can return to gender-based standards, and allow women to enter the infantry with lower standards than men. They have tried both. And, always, in the background are generals and commanders ask-ing leading questions like: "Why don't we have more women in combat roles? Why are so many women failing?" While posited as a question, subordinates hear exactly what it is: a directive. And they scramble duti-fully. So, whether it's Ranger School in the Army or Marine infantry units, women are treated differently—whether the policy directs that standard or not.

Take the Army's Airborne School as an example. Women have long attended Airborne School, but now that women in infantry units need to attend the course, the standards have changed. The daily five-mile run, long a staple, has disappeared. It was never a formal "standard," but instead a tough aspect of the course that weeded out weaker candi-dates. Too many women were washing out, so the run went away. They also used to foot-march to the hangar before jumps—now students are bused. Are either of these traditions tied to jumping out of airplanes? Maybe not, but they reinforced the challenge of graduating Airborne School. Too many women were falling out, so the physical demands were diminished. This is happening in course after course, training after training, across our military. Take this to the bank: Every *single* mili-

THE WAR ON WARRIORS

tary training course in the name of gender "equity" is getting softer and easier. As is our military—softer and easier . . . to defeat.

But at least we have more ponytails in our formations! On women— and men!

Does any of it make for stronger, tougher, better-trained soldiers? The question answers itself.

Because it's impossible, the Army has been unable to find a gender-neutral "standard." They even announced a fundamental overhaul of the Army Physical Fitness Test (APFT) in 2018, which has been a failure. Not only is the new test extremely arduous to administer at the unit level, but the test is actually more grueling—which means, you guessed it, it's even more difficult to have male/female parity. So, you guessed it too, politicians and generals put downward pressure on physical standard. Today, the minimum standard of push-ups for a female in the Army, age twenty-two to twenty-six, is eleven. *Eleven.* Minimum standard for a two-mile run? Twenty-one minutes.

Bobby, meet the new member of your infantry squad. She can do ten push-ups at a pop and run at a brisk ten-minute mile. *Get motivated!*

My old First Sergeant Eric Geressy—one of the toughest warriors I have ever known—was recently a sergeant major at US Southern Command. He has almost thirty years of Army experience and shares a double-barreled take on women in the Army:

"If you go back to Panama, there was an MP female company commander who got maximum press coverage. This was back in 1989. Wasn't made into a big deal. Then Jessica Lynch. They turned her into a hero. Even though she says that she didn't do shit. Bronze Star medal. Big hero. That was Bush and Rumsfeld. It's both parties with this nonsense. It got started when they started pushing females into these roles, around 2005. They pushed forward support companies up into infantry battalions. That was new when I was with 3-187 [the unit where I served with Geressy]. They filled so many positions with females that we were short with combat medics. I had to staff clinics with female medics, so you could push males into the line units. None of this had anything to do with warfighting. I used to think, if we got into a big war . . . the chicken shit would go away. Instead, it accelerated."

SGM Geressy is referring to the early era of the Iraq War when forward support companies (FSCs)—logistics units that were added to infantry battalions—were a backdoor way for women into combat. What we all knew was that in an asymmetrical war there were no front lines. All soldiers were in combat. In reality, what we learned was simple: Jessica Lynch, like most female soldiers at that time, was untrained and unprepared.

"From my perspective, overwhelmingly most females want nothing to do with combat arms. They aren't showing up in droves. I'm not a fucking marketing expert, but no shit, Sherlock," Geressy said.

Even the award process becomes political, noted SGM Geressy: "One female medic in the 82nd Airborne, they gave her a Silver Star in Afghanistan in 2008. Monica Brown. They had her picture posted everywhere. Her picture posted at the military balls, in garrison, in the chow hall. Award given by Vice President Dick Cheney. Why is that? None of my guys had their picture on the wall. And LeeAnn Hester. She got a silver star for actions in Iraq in March of 2005. She got the award in June—it only took three months." Nothing happens that fast . . . unless there is an agenda.

SGM Geressy was an infantryman's infantryman. Admired by all who served with him and under him. The man has been to every armpit and butthole in the world, with a ballistic plate on his chest and smoking rifle in hand. He was awarded a Silver Star that took over eighteen months to be approved. The Silver Star is the second-highest valor award bestowed for combat valor by the United States Army. He received the award from a mail clerk at the Sergeant Major Academy. Nobody gave a shit. They mailed it to him. No picture in the chow hall for this warrior.

If SGM Geressy was a transvestite—or gay, or black, or a woman—he would have three Distinguished Service Crosses and be on the front of a Wheaties box. *Get motivated!*

Brian Relation is a Green Beret Master Sergeant (MSG). He did five deployments in his first five years in Army special forces. He then became a tactics instructor for three years with one deployment in between. He then went back to the SF teams and did four more overseas deployments. MSG Relation deployed ten total times for his country. I'd say, to say the least, that he punched his ticket. He also instructed ROTC at two major universities.

"There are three female Green Berets. One is transgender. One shot a hole through the wall. One seems to be legit. I knew her instructors and they thought she was great. That being said, I don't think women should be a part of special ops. They should not be in combat. All the studies confirm that—but we deny what we see with our eyes. I have met some high-speed females that can do legit stuff. But you can't go to a Muslim country with a female on your team. They will reject it. So what's the point?" MSG Relation told me.

MSG Relation fought Al Qaeda and the Taliban in Afghanistan. In one deployment they took out 26 of the 126 most violent and wanted terrorists in the world. But he soon realized the biggest danger to his career was female cadets at ROTC at American stateside universities.

"I came into work one day and they hit me with, 'Were you touching a girl inappropriately?' I was like, 'You mean the girl that I helped with leg tucks for the new PT test?' Two other female cadets reported me, even though the girl had asked for help and she wasn't even the one who claimed I did anything to her. I want nothing to do with that nonsense."

As I mentioned, in October 2022, the Army introduced a new fitness standard called the Army Combat Fitness Test (ACFT), a test that doesn't seem to benefit the argument of women serving at the same standard as men. MSG Relation told me in an interview, "With the new ACFT, physical standards have gone completely out the window. The ACFT itself will make for a fatter and less fit standard. But the women really struggle on the most basic tasks."

MSG Relation shared a story about Air Assault School, an Army qualification school that trains soldiers in repelling, assaulting from helicopters, and sling loading. "Zero day [day before they start training] they had a rainstorm. PT [physical training] test, obstacle course, boot run, etc. They started with 330 people and dropped down to 126 before school started. Because of adverse conditions. The reality of combat, in training. All the women quit. Is it a weaker/softer generation? Was it the conditions? Or was it because they just couldn't cut it?"

* * *

In today's military—ask anyone still serving or recently separated—our soldiers are fatter and slower. It doesn't help that 77 percent of military-age Americans do not qualify for military service due to weight issues, medical problems, drug use, or a criminal background. This is true, and DoD recruiting makes this excuse every single day. But it's only part of the military recruitment story.

For those still eligible, in order to be more inclusive for all genders (biological and supposed), we lower the standards. The United States Air Force in January 2023 lowered their height and weight standards again—they had to. They changed the "tape" standard, otherwise known as the Body Composition Assessment. This evaluated an Airman's obesity by using a tape measure to compare height to circumference measurements around the hips to determine overall body fat. When Airmen (and the new Space Force Guardians!) don't meet the new standard, they won't be punished. They will be enrolled into a "Body Composition Improvement Program" for twelve months and referred to their on-base medical treatment facility for an exam to determine whether they're at risk for any health issues. Also, while I was writing this book, the Air Force dropped the requirement for high school or GED diplomas for new recruits. No more high school degrees needed.

Simply put: we are lowering the standard for everyone in the name of promoting women, fat people, and now high school dropouts. Our so-called military leaders, obsessed with recruiting and retention problems of their own making, don't want anyone with a pulse prevented from joining or being pushed out of the military. A quick reminder: unlike in the civilian world, when you suck at your combat job, you literally can get a sucking chest wound from multiple gunshots or lose a leg from a hidden IED. Somehow that gets missed in all this feel good, inclusive ass-hattery.

The standard should be . . . drum roll, please . . . the same standard for everyone. But if we are going to maintain gender-based standards, then you have to tier it by military occupational specialty (MOS). Want to be in the infantry? The standards will be higher for both men and women. Want to work a desk job? Ten push-ups will suffice. Want to fly drones? It's okay that you're a little fatter, but you'd better have twenty-twenty vision. The examples go on and on.

The problem the gender cultists have with this is that, yes, it will mean very few women qualify for the infantry, and more generals asking, "Why are so many women failing?" And the cycle continues. Politicians with bad ideas (and bad intentions), and feckless generals coming to heel.

They have forgotten their oath. They don't want to attempt to see the world from anywhere but their windowless room at the Pentagon. *Harvard does this, Stanford does this, why can't we do this?*

* * *

But why should we be surprised? These same morally bankrupt minds are just doing what they always do: preaching, reality be damned. Social justice for everyone, everywhere! They are pushing the same things on our own troops that they pushed on foreign populations. The utopian goal of "democracy" in the Middle East was possible, if only we taught enough women's studies to a culture in Afghanistan that is 50/50 on female castration and female literacy. Equality in these parts of the world tends to tilt more toward the Code of Hammurabi than the California Assembly. Yet the Obama/Biden State Department dove headfirst into the shallow end of the pond with social justice policies doomed to fail, while stamping their feet that modernizing a culture begins with implementing diversity training before indoor plumbing and localized security can begin. We have met the enemy, and it is us—and now it is coming for Private Joe Snuffy.

If the politicians and generals simply ignore the results of their own tests, then how can we ever expect them to take responsibility for their own actions? Sending men, and now women, into combat is a sacred and sobering responsibility. Sending women into combat without the proper readiness for the tasks before them will create a generation of sacrificial lambs to the slaughter in combat zones and in homes across the nation. Sending women into combat while gaslighting them into believing that the Ring of Gloria Allred will protect them from danger is not just reckless, it's sinful. When bullets ping and whine over your head, the only standard that matters is the cyclic rate of machine gun fire. Anything else you tell yourself is a lie.

You can cook the books and massage the findings in the pages of the *Washington Post* or for the listeners of NPR, but once these units see combat and the casualties mount, will those who advocated these experiments take responsibility for their actions? I would guess they will once again blame the NCOs and the military without ever remembering the debates of those who warned against these actions. Forgotten will be the fact that our armed forces were forced to accept the political manipulation of our infantry units for blue state approval and cheers from the so-called enlightened classes, who are actually idiots.

But women also get a vote, and they are voting with their feet. Retention for women in the military is declining. Turns out, as my former first sergeant pointed out, the majority of women want *nothing* to do with the prospect of being in combat—let alone actual combat. So how does the Biden administration's Defense Department deal with that issue? Abortion.

The Post Millennial, a conservative news site, broke the story in 2023 when it exposed a series of training videos from the US Department of Veterans Affairs that are using mental health as a justification for the VA to pay for abortions of veterans and active-duty females serving in the military. According to the new policy, the real purpose of these abortions is *retention*, continuing female military careers by helping them end unwanted pregnancies.

The military and VA try to say, without making eye contact, that this is all about mental health. *Sure.* Their lying logic: we must protect the mental health of women in the military. This helps win wars. We are better prepared for Russia and China, and it helps female careerism.

Our military now trains our metaphorical life givers to be combat life takers, and then when they become biological life givers, our DoD and VA help them be baby life takers in the name of keeping them on the team as combat life takers. The logic . . . of evil.

When the Supreme Court struck down *Roe v. Wade* in the summer of 2022, the Biden administration frothed into a panic and took steps to work around the near forty-year moratorium on government-funded abortions at both the VA and the Department of Defense.

The DoD was silent when Senator Roger Wicker (R-MS) asked what the actual number was of women getting abortions covered by taxpayers while serving in the military. According to sources under oath, this seems to be something that we can never possibly calculate. It is a great unknown to the Department of Defense.

Like the origin of life. The existence of aliens. Or the source of cocaine at the White House. We will never know.

The VA health system is a little more forthcoming, and the number of female veterans seeking abortions is off the charts. Of the almost one million females in the VA health system, nearly 18 percent have sought at least one abortion.

Thank you for serving our country—now we will help you kill your unborn child.

The VA wants you to know that this isn't about politics or an agenda; this is about the children of female soldiers and veterans. (At least the children that are not aborted with your taxpayer dollars.) The children of mothers with PTSD are at greater risk for significant negative health outcomes, including preterm birth, low birth weight, and long-term emotional problems.

"Mental health conditions in general are associated with increased rates of pregnancy complications, and when we look at the two diagnoses that are most common among women veterans, PTSD and depression, we see a really sizable influence." The VA video was titled "Mental Health and Abortion."

The VA contends that female veterans with PTSD are more likely to have issue or complex pregnancies, higher rates of gestational diabetes, and preeclampsia. So you are probably better off just, you know, aborting them. And we can keep more women in the military. And we can, of course, defeat ISIS and free Ukraine.

Few doctors will go on record recommending abortion for these reasons, but that isn't important to the DoD or the VA under President Joe Biden. More women must serve, mental health, abortion, and unit readiness be damned.

They claim that "mental health" and PTSD are not the only reasons that veterans need free abortions. There is of course the "fear of reprimand" when they get pregnant (usually that happens right after deployment orders are cut). Of course, nothing ruins a deployment like when you get pregnant. Some females in the military say that they have a hard time doing "certain jobs" while pregnant. *Shocking.* All the more reason, in the minds of agenda-driven leftists, to fund abortion for the VA and DoD.

Abortion is not between a doctor and a woman (and I define woman as a person who is actually a woman). It is now a decision made between her doctor, her therapist, herself, her veteran advocate, and her first-line supervisor in the military.

Who could possibly argue with that logic?

* * *

Here's more logic for you. In July 2023, President Biden had to replace the outgoing chief of naval operations. The Associated Press and *Politico* ran stories that the president would name Admiral Samuel Paparo. He was the head of the Pacific Fleet. Paparo was the tip of the spear of all Indo-Pacific Navy leadership. This is China, Taiwan, North Korea, and every other major news story having anything to do with boats or the US Navy for the last six years. Paparo was a combat veteran who was in charge of all the global action the Navy was involved in pacifying. He also came with recommendations from his secretary of the Navy and Secretary of Defense Lloyd Austin. Seems like the media had been tipped off as to who Joe Biden would name as the chief of naval operations.

Honorably mentioned in this story was Admiral Lisa Franchetti. She would be the first female CNO but she had no combat experience. Admiral Franchetti got her master's degree from the University of Phoenix online. So much for the Ivy League elitists. There were other factors going against her too. The CNO has almost never gone to the vice chief in decades; rather they promote the freshest commander. And let's be honest, this is President Biden. Franchetti was not a *trans* woman, and that could be a strike against her in this administration.

But no, Biden shocked the world when he went with another inexperienced first, promoting Franchetti. If naval operations suffers, at least we can hold our heads high. Because at least we have another *first*! The first female member of the Joint Chiefs of Staff—hooray.

For social justice ideologues, PR matters more than reality. Politics is all about optics instead of results. Naval operations being weakened won't matter to anyone in the legacy media. In the world of *Annie Get Your Gun*, "anything you can do, I can do better." It's a great number in a musical that grossly exaggerates the mythical performance of a traveling western entertainment sharpshooter who reads dialogue back in the nineteenth century.

War isn't about inclusion. It's not about safety and empathy. It's the terrible reality that exists when all law and order has broken down, and the only thing left is force. In that time, the goal must be winning—and reality. Not public relations.

The media and the elites will proclaim the valor of the next Joan of Arc as she is bloodied and tortured. They will tell us about bravery and progress. They will erect statues and commission awards. Movie studios will pay the families of the dead for the rights to have Zendaya star in the big-budget film. No one will ask why we did this or if this was a good idea.

The blood of America's daughters will be on their hands.

Chapter 6

THE ARMY THINKS THE ENEMY . . . IS PETE

As I mentioned briefly in the introduction to this book, my final Army "deployment" was not overseas—it was here at home, in our nation's capital. In June 2020, after deployments in Cuba, Iraq, and Afghanistan, I held a riot shield outside the White House, clashing with BLM rioters and Antifa anarchists. More on this later in the book.

But, at the time, I lived in New Jersey and worked in New York City. So how did I end up in the DC National Guard, defending the White House? It was a four-hour drive just to report to duty. Why DC?

Funny you should ask.

When I rejoined the National Guard in 2019—after five years in the Individual Ready Reserve (basically my name on an Army list)—I had planned to join my old infantry battalion in New York City: the Fighting 69th. Storied history, great soldiers, and I'd been in the unit before. I also didn't want to be in a higher headquarters unit—that's why I got out of the Army in 2014. Higher headquarters crush your soul. They are bureaucratic, political, and mind-numbingly boring. I wanted to get back out on the gun range, back on the drill floor, out with soldiers.

I knew there weren't many jobs in infantry battalions for majors. Maybe two or three. But, thankfully, my good friend—whom I went to the Captain's Career Course with at Fort Knox, Kentucky—was the new battalion commander of the Fighting 69th. Great dude. I called him up. He was thrilled to have me. He said they could easily get me into the unit—even if they had to create an additional slot. Routine stuff, and he'd make it happen. He had never had a request like this denied.

I was pumped. I could serve near my house, the unit got an experienced soldier, and—based on my civilian job—I could probably get the unit some good publicity. It was a win-win-win. A no-brainer.

Until.

Just a few days before initiating the transfer into the unit, and the New York National Guard, I got a call from my battalion commander friend. He was pained. He hesitated. I could tell he was embarrassed. He spoke in code.

I couldn't join the unit. They had denied my slot. He had *never* seen this happen before. He didn't name names but said it came from "the very top."

Pete Hegseth is not wanted in the New York National Guard.

It had been a done deal. Now it was . . . done.

I asked why. He wasn't given a reason, at least not at that time. As I was writing this book, I asked him again. This time, he didn't miss a beat:

"Pete, I can confirm, one hundred percent, that the division commander wanted you in the unit. And I've never seen him get overruled. He runs the division. But he was overruled. The adjutant general [TAG] of New York—General Ray Shields—shot it down. It was made clear by him—and told directly to me: Pete Hegseth will not serve in our unit."

My buddy continued: "Who's his boss? Governor Andrew Cuomo. So, you guessed it. It's political."

Fuck Cuomo.

So I can't serve in an infantry unit—serve the country and the state—because I have a different political persuasion? I was pissed, but there was nothing I could do about it. So I went looking for other units. Someone recommended a specialized unit in Washington, DC. It was a headquarters unit. *Dammit.*

With that, I ended up in the most political unit in the Army—the DC National Guard. It wasn't where I wanted to be, but it's where I was—and we had a job to do.

As a member of the DC National Guard, our unit was tasked with supporting the inauguration of the president. We protect the parade routes, as well as crowd control of the events in our nation's capital. In January 2021, for the inauguration of President-elect Joe Biden, I was given orders to serve in Washington, DC, from the Monday to the Friday of that week; then I would host my show *FOX & Friends* in New York City that Saturday. It was extraordinary times, but I was just an ordinary soldier. Following the events of January 6, this inauguration was all-hands-on-deck. *Everyone* in the DC Guard was mobilized, along with tens of thousands of guardsmen from other states.

Everybody knew I wasn't a Biden fan, but that didn't matter. I had served in uniform under Bush, Obama, Trump, and now Biden. Defending the inauguration would be a first for me, but an extension of service.

Until.

Again, until.

Just one day prior to reporting for duty—out of the blue—I received a call from my unit leadership that I was to "stand down" and that I was "not needed." My orders had been revoked. They said that they were "good on numbers" and that I was no longer needed for duty. My orders had been revoked. Remember, at this time, after January 6, 2021, we had over 25,000 troops guarding Washington, DC, and no one was allowed to be relieved. Yet my leadership told me that I was not needed. Twenty-five thousand other soldiers had to deploy to DC for five months, but I was told to relax.

This was not my first rodeo. I'd never had orders revoked. I knew this was nonsense. This duty was mandatory. One of the few things the DC Guard does that actually *is* mandatory. We had elected officials and CNN (falsely) claiming that Proud Boys and Oath Keepers were coming to finish the job at the inauguration. They had National Guard troops sleeping in parking garages in the bitter cold of a DC winter and I was told that everyone was needed . . . except me.

At first, I was confused.

Then I was pissed-off.

Fuck Mark Milley too.

No one said a word to me all week. Nobody would, or could. No peers. No commanders. Not even subordinates. I figured the tempo and the high-profile nature of the events surrounding DC required everyone to focus on the mission at hand. But I couldn't shake this feeling in my stomach. It was the strangest feeling, like my foundations had shifted—leaving me out of balance. I spoke to my wife, Jenny, about it and we both had the exact same response. Something else was going on. All was not as it appeared.

FOX News alert: I am pro-Trump. Everybody knew that before I joined the DC National Guard, and didn't have a problem with it. In fact, most of my fellow soldiers—even in DC—felt the same way. Frankly, so did most of the military—especially combat arms. President Trump was, and is, beloved by warfighters. He funded them, untied their hands, didn't use them unnecessarily, and let them win.

But then January 6 happened, and Joe Biden was on his way in. The entire paradigm had shifted. And so, even though I had rejoined the National Guard in 2019 to continue serving, something was off. I couldn't go back to a unit that didn't need me when it needed soldiers the most. They turned their back on me. The message was clear: you are not wanted here.

So, I resigned.

On January 20, 2021, I drafted the letter. *Fuck Biden anyway.*

My last day in uniform was March 31, 2021.

After a few years in the IRR—with an email notification—I was officially separated from the Army on January 1, 2024.

Three deployments, fourteen years in uniform, awards, decorations, glowing evaluation reports. And it was over.

I would miss the Army, but not the DC National Guard.

But what was the *real* reason my orders were revoked to help guard the inauguration? The question irked me, long after leaving the unit. When I left, I left it all behind. I didn't ask questions; I just got the hell out. But now—while writing this book, I had to know.

So I called a senior leader in the unit and asked him, "Sir, will you just give me the real reason I was not invited to Biden's inauguration?"

There was a long pause over the phone. Then breathing.

Man, this must be bad. It must be what I thought.

The leader said to me, "Look, Major, I know with ninety-nine point nine-nine percent certainty because I was in the meetings and on the emails."

He paused again, as if that was all I needed to know. I wanted more, so I pushed.

"Okay, sir. What happened?"

"Okay, so, you were not brought to the inauguration because they dubbed you an extremist."

He stopped. Started again. And then hesitated.

"You were not brought to the inauguration because . . . they dubbed you as a white nationalist and an extremist. You got flagged by two soldiers who had been trolling your social media. They saw your tattoo. And the tattoo was what they flagged you on."

"I have many tattoos. Which one made them say that? This is outrageous."

"Yeah, well, Major Hegseth. It is quite absurd. The cross on your chest was what they determined was what made you an extremist and domestic threat. That cross, it was determined, is a tattoo of a white nationalist extremist."

"It's a Jerusalem Cross! Did they even google it?!"

The Jerusalem Cross represents Christ's sacrifice and the mission to spread his gospel to the four corners of the world. There is one large cross in the middle and four smaller crosses at each corner. This was part of the coat of arms after AD 1203 and the 104-year reign of the Jerusalem Kingdom. I got it after I saw it on a church while walking the streets of Jerusalem.

It's a religious symbol, not a white nationalist symbol. Yet my detractors made the argument that I was a threat, a racist, and an extremist; not qualified to guard the inauguration. I was told that a few of my unit leaders tried to stand up for me, but it was futile. The DC Army National Guard leadership was clear: block him. As was relayed to me later, they literally said, "Hegseth needs to stay the fuck away."

Just like New York, Hegseth needs to stay the fuck away.

But was this really about a cross? Was this really about one Christian man? A Christian man with no history of doing anything extreme other than doing what he was told in the Army and serving his country? What can one Christian man do to dismantle their agenda? Maybe a lot . . . I guess we'll find out after this book.

Maybe it was too many crosses? Would just one cross be okay? Or does the Army think that all white Christians are white nationalists? Is it all Christians? All whites? All Trump supporters? Or is it just Pete Hegseth? The reason given to me was "the cross on my chest," but we all know it was much more than that. The problem was who I was, what I believed, certainly who I worked for, and the political candidate I supported. This story is about a lot more than Pete Hegseth.

* * *

Three overseas deployments. Fourteen years in uniform. Trained and ready. Combat experience.

Until . . . I was labeled an extremist and my career was over . . . because two senior Army leaders with an agenda trolled my Instagram for pictures of my family on vacation.

And nobody showed the courage to do something about it.

The Department of Defense dubbed me an extremist because I put a Jerusalem Cross on my chest signifying to the world that I am an unapologetic follower of my Lord and Savior Jesus Christ. Oh, and I'm also a supporter of Donald Trump. So *clearly* I can't be trusted to defend an inauguration of an opposing party.

Yes, I have a problem with what people like Mark Milley, Lloyd Austin, and Bishop Garrison are doing to the military. Not to my military. *Our* military. Our nation. My situation was emblematic of all these other soldiers who were checked and flagged for extremism. But I was fortunate, I was able to get an explanation. Without this book—and my ability to dig, thanks to my rank and my position in the media—I would never know what actually happened. Nobody was going to tell me. Instead, they tried to hide it. They just wanted me away from the inauguration and out of the unit. Most other soldiers— quietly dubbed "extremists"—never find out how, or why, such things happened to them.

Extremism.

For what?

If they can do that to a guy who is on national television on the most-watched cable news station on the planet, they will do it to anyone, for any reason. I tattooed my chest to show that my religion is front and center in my life. I am a husband, a father, and a soldier because of my relationship with Christ. My faith is what I want closest to my heart.

At least now we know what we're up against. I certainly do and found out personally. I fought religious extremists for over twenty years in uniform. Then I was accused of being one.

What we're facing here is a fundamentally different view of what we stand for. For the Left, if something is normal or traditional, it's bad. Will they do the actual work to explain why a tattoo is bad? No way.

The Left today wants to have it both ways—more beta/soft men who don't conform to traditional gender roles *and* a military of young people willing and able to defend the country. That doesn't work. Nor does the inverse: America is still full of young, strong, alpha males who love their country and want to defend their family *but* those young males see a military that doesn't want to recruit them. So, you get what the hard Left really wants—soft men, and a weak military. Neutered at home and neutered abroad.

While I was writing this book, the Army started (once again) producing television commercials that featured mostly white men (gasp!)

doing tough things and taking risks. The type of ads that actually tap into the sense of honor and heroism that healthy young men aspire to. My phone was quickly inundated with text messages from veterans with one message: *must be time to go to war again!*

For the past three years, the Pentagon—across all branches—has embraced the social justice messages of gender equity, racial diversity, climate stupidity, vaccine worship, and the LGBTQA+ alphabet soup in their recruiting pushes. Only one problem: there just aren't enough trannies from Brooklyn or lesbians from San Francisco who want to join the 82nd Airborne. Not only do the trannies and lesbians not join, but those very same ads turn off the young, patriotic, Christian men who have traditionally filled our ranks.

The Left scorns these men, but America needs them. Black, white, rich, poor, rural, urban—America needs our strong men to defend us.

You know who recruits "heroic men" very well these days—Antifa and Black Lives Matter, among other militant left-wing causes. I carried a riot shield and stared across from them outside Lafayette Square. They may be miseducated about God and country, but that does not erase their genetic makeup. These are men. These are brave men. They risk life, limb, and reputation to fight against . . . well, God and country. They are instinctively ready and willing to fight . . . but for what? Whatever they are conditioned to think is worth fighting for—or against. And if all of our society, schools, and government tell them America is bad, then they will righteously (or so they think) take up arms against big, bad America. More on this in a moment. . . .

Thankfully, there are still more of "us" than "them." The Antifa activists are loud but they're also masked, skinny, and marginalized. Across America, from small town to small town, there are still hundreds of thousands of patriotic, strong, manly men ripe for recruitment. The military just needs to speak to them, and then stand beside them. They will give their lives for this country, but this country—and our military—has to show that it values them first.

The Left today—weaponized inside the DoD—is not just ideologically slanted. This is dogma. This is religious fundamentalism. This is a religion to these woke zealots. And they have been tasked with purging the ranks of those who do not bow to their government god.

They got me . . . for now.

But this is not just the targeting of our active duty and our reservists; they even started to go after the children of service members at DoD schools.

Kelisa Wing was a Diversity, Equity, and Inclusion chief at the Pentagon's educational department, called the DoDEA, the Department of Defense Education Activity. They teach all students of service members at DoD schools. She was involved in constructing a curriculum for over 60,000 military-connected children at over 150 schools across the planet. Hired in December 2021, her questionable past was initially highlighted by FOX News and other outlets. Wing had endorsed a "social justice" book for children in elementary classrooms that labeled first responders of September 11, 2001, "menaces." Forget that the Pentagon itself lost 125 souls that day and 59 that died on American Airlines Flight 77.

Kelisa Wing promoted the antipolice book *Between the World and Me*, by Ta-Nehisi Coates, while on the job as the Pentagon's educational department. This was a book where the author Coates writes of the first responders of 9/11, "They were not human to me. Black, white, or whatever, they were menaces of nature; they were the fire, the comet, the storm, which could—with no justification—shatter my body."

The Pentagon, under Secretary Austin and General Milley, hired a "defund the police" zealot who would spend her time indoctrinating the children of service members that police should be defunded and abolished.

She later got attention for tweeting, ". . . this lady actually had the CAUdacity to say that black people can be racist too . . . I had to stop the session and give Karen the BUSINESS . . . we are not the majority, we don't have power."

If you're not tracking with her sharp and original wit, "Caudacity" is a slang term that is used to describe audacity demonstrated by white people or Caucasians.

On another occasion, Wing responded to a user who said, "I am exhausted by 99% of the white men in education and 95% of the white women. Where can I get a break from white nonsense for a while?"

As a result of these tweets, as well as the books she coauthored, twenty-two House Republicans—including some on the Armed Services Committee—requested that Secretary of Defense Austin take "immediate action" to investigate Wing for "egregious bias."

Yet the director of DoDEA, Thomas Brady, said, "Kelisa Wing is exactly the right person to lead our efforts in building on the foundational work done to support meaningful change in our organization." *Exactly* the right person.

The truth is that we will never convert the Kelisa Wings and the Bishop Garrisons to our way of thinking. We will never embarrass them enough to get them to stop tweeting and writing statements that, if the skin color or pronouns were reversed, would be recognized as straight up racist. Our only chance is to expose them and get them fired. And then elect a commander in chief who would *never* allow their ideological likes to be hired ever again.

Those who push DEI/CRT ideology are not approaching these topics as research scientists in lab coats or even social scientists with data-driven research or cross-cultural "controls" on their conclusions. They have deliberately ignored the racism and the bigotry of America's enemies in the Middle East for the past twenty years. They try to shut down the Masters golf tournament in Augusta, Georgia, because of its racist past, yet say nary a word when the Saudi Arabian government buys the PGA. They seek reparations for those whose distant relatives suffered through slavery in the early nineteenth century, yet they promote world leaders who currently enslave their own citizens to create cheap labor for the mining of minerals and the assembly of circuit boards. They take obvious positions mocking peaceful Christianity but somehow celebrate the virtues of citizen-killing Chairman Mao and sword-wielding Muhammad. In their fevered minds it doesn't matter if you are a murderer; it just matters if you murder the wrong ethnic group.

None of what they proclaim rises to the level of intellectual evidence. They are demanding that the world accept their controversial and unproven assertions about the root causes of violence, failure, abuse, crime, and poverty. They are Marxists, and so do all these things without evidence and without humility. Furthermore, they are not simply asking for us to consider their ideas; they are demanding that we change our laws, codes, and legal expectations based on unproven and provocative ideological theories.

You know what they are? They're traitors. Plain and simple. And our constitutional responsibility is to expose them, remove them, and defeat what they stand for.

They are transforming the American military in their own radical image—and the Pentagon leadership, from Secretary Austin to Chairman Milley, back them all the way. Cowards with stars, complicit as they laud the enemy within.

With free speech as our First Amendment, America is a country founded on not criminalizing wrong thoughts or wrong speech, it was founded to make illegal wrong actions. Here's the point: in the hands of the military and with the application of the full force of the uniform military code to push their agenda, those who seek to retrain soldiers on what they *think* or *believe* are guilty of coercive violence against their neighbors. It's happening right now, up and down our ranks.

One of the most important books written in the last ten years dealing with this very topic is John McWhorter's *Woke Racism: How a New Religion Has Betrayed Black America.* McWhorter, himself a black man, writes about the new religion of woke racists. He offers solutions that our military and all citizens of the nation should consider when engaged in the fight against DEI/CRT, correctly noting that in such times, we cannot be afraid of unjust accusations:

> *What we must do . . . is stand up to them. They rule by inflecting terror. They think that to require them to engage in actual reason is heretically white. There is nowhere to go with them from there. Our response to this can't be to simply fold because this means giving up the post enlightenment society we hold dear. We must stop being afraid of these people, and once we do there is something we need to steel ourselves against and get used to. . . . They WILL call you a racist. No matter what you do or say beyond what they stipulate as proper.*

The underlying point of McWhorter's strategy is that you can't argue with people who don't believe truth exists. You're not playing by the same rules. The only solution is a rock-solid sense of self. Forget compliance; the only response to an unfair standard is noncompliance, grounded in integrity. McWhorter outlines this new world, reminding us of the value of maverick thinking:

> *The coping strategy therefore must be not to try to avoid letting them call you a racist but to get used to their doing so and walk on despite it. Specifically, on top of all else we are required to manage,*

enlightened Americans must be accustomed to being called racist in the public square. We must become more comfortable keeping our own counsel and letting our own rationality decide whether we are racist, rather than entertaining the eccentric self-serving, renovated definitions of racism forced upon us by religionists. When that type calls you a racist, and I mean white ones every bit as black ones, you need not walk off doing the work of wondering whether your accuser was right. You are Galileo being told not to make sense because the Bible doesn't like it.

We have a big problem, and it's metastasizing. For a long time now, most American children in government schools have not been taught history, patriotism, or anything about God, let alone the Christian God that informed our founding. It has been just the opposite: they have been taught about what a horrible racist country we are. Since most people don't want to be horrible racists or support horrible racists, why would they sign up to fight for such a country? Or, knowing they are not racist, why would they sign up for a military that sees them as the *new* second-class citizens? So they don't join. They skip military service, understandably so. And the militant Left gets more of what they want.

Yet, still, there they are. America's sons and daughters on watch. Walking patrol. They miss sleep to not miss the enemy's probe. They don't eat because the enemy approaches fast and on their own terms. They stand on guard, cold, because the only way to fight the enemy is to fight where you are not expected to fight. A generation of good, young, patriotic Americans who are strong, independent thinkers who do love what this country was supposed to stand for. But there are fewer and fewer of them.

No wonder there is a massive recruiting crisis in our military today—especially from young white men. Why would God-fearing, traditional, patriotic kids be excited about dodging accusations of racism and then deciding on pronouns before jumping into a foxhole with a "man" who is more concerned about becoming a woman than being a warrior? It used to be army green—all in this together. Now it's urban camo—that ugly black, white, and gray camouflage. We are seen, like yesteryear, by our skin color—black, white, or otherwise. And the gray area, that's where the Left pushes everything else—driving black and white soldiers into their corners, pitting male and female against each other—when they should be back-to-back, guns out, together.

The military was not built for radical social engineering but—when weaponized—is tragically good at it. We can no longer expect to win the wars our nation sends us to fight if the sniper fire is coming from inside our ranks, and straight from the front of our formations.

Chapter 7

RIOT SHIELDS AND *REAL* RACISM

Riot shields surrounded me. Most were smeared with the filth of the streets and covered in the greasy handprints of America's youth. A pitiful collage of images that brought to mind my own kids' Father's Day school art project stenciled with their tiny palms. The protective crowd-control gear was scattered on the ground of the armory drill floor. I stepped around the dispersed debris to choose one that looked sturdy. I picked one that was relatively clean on its surface, but upon further inspection, the inside made me reject it. While clean on the outside, the interior of the shield was streaked in pink, a combination of blood and sweat of the person who had previously used it for its defense—a testament to the violence that it had seen and the injury that it had witnessed.

The DC National Guard Armory was due east of the U.S. Capitol Building. Outside it smelled like an aromatherapy diffuser filled with weed and pepper spray. Inside, the armory had a pungent odor reminiscent of a high school locker room. Discarded socks and desiccated sweat. Vanquished foot powders and deodorizers hanging in the air in the attempt to cut the overwhelming odors decaying in a makeshift locker room of a team as maligned and unappreciated as the Washington Generals.

Normally, an Army major walking around inspecting equipment would draw some attention. Normal times. These were far from normal times. Five days earlier, on May 25, 2020, in the middle of the hundred-years pandemic of COVID-19, a local police enforcement action in my (former) home state of Minnesota lit a powder keg of simmering racial hostility.

George Floyd, a clearly troubled man with a long history of legal issues, primarily caused by his personal demons and addictions, lost his life while resisting arrest under the custody of a white Minneapolis police officer (subsequent revelations have shown it was drugs, not a knee, that killed Floyd). The death of George Floyd, which was broadcast to the world from cell phone video footage, sparked protests and riots across the entirety of the United States of America. The audio of Floyd yelling "I can't breathe!" instantly resonated with those who believed from personal experience, or educational expectations, that America was a helplessly racist nation. Responses to the video provided the media and disgruntled young people with a litmus test that would draw the boldest racial lines in a generation.

COVID isolation, Trump hatred in an election year, and the perceived racism of Red State America provided the progressive Left and its allies in the media with the perfect environment to foment chaos. Young people locked down by an abundance of (false) caution, but really just control, found the perfect outlet for their cabin fever. "Black Lives Matter" riots would define the summer of 2020.

Young people—but especially young men—always need an outlet for pursuing heroic action. Americans embracing that risk-taking, passionate instinct have led the country to make great strides through history. What I saw that week in Washington, DC, was all of those passions expressed in the worst way possible.

* * *

Under the guise of "justice," hundreds of thousands of demonstrators across the country started attacking law enforcement officers, causing city and state leadership to mobilize their National Guard troops to provide security for businesses that had been burned and looted in the chaos. As national leaders watched images of George Floyd's death in rhythm with cities burning and cops bleeding, the inclination to call active-duty military troops into our American cities gained momentum.

Our nation's capital was front and center to these "Black Lives Matter" protests. On May 29, days after the death of George Floyd, waves of violent professional agitators (led by Antifa members) infiltrated otherwise mostly peaceful George Floyd protestors in Washington, DC. By the time the sun set on May 29 the situation in our nation's capital had risen to the level of a national crisis.

Not since August 1814, when Major General Robert Ross marched his victorious British soldiers from Bladensburg, Maryland, into Washington City and razed the White House home of President James Madison, had there been a more serious threat to our nation's capital.

If January 6, 2021, was an insurrection, then surely this was too.

Hundreds of violent protestors attacked the makeshift barricades erected by White House security staff. The Secret Service showed almost reckless disregard for the lives they protect, allowing the exterior gates north of the White House through Lafayette Park to be breached numerous times by rioters. Scared to face backlash, the defenders refused to deploy force. By sunup, sixty Secret Service officers had been wounded and eleven were held in hospitals. The Secret Service, nearly overwhelmed by the numbers of the protestors and the speed with which they mobilized, eventually prevailed and locked down the White House. They had succeeded in fulfilling their mandate to protect the most powerful man in the world, who was secured by armed agents in an undisclosed location on the premises. This assault on the White House was met by the national media with jeers and disrespect not for the rioters, but for the administration and its defenders in the Secret Service. It was Trump, after all, so all bets were off.

DC mayor Muriel Bowser, already a political foil of President Trump, wasted no time using this as another attempt to curry favor with her rabid base, even as her city came apart at the seams. Trump, with direct supervision over the secretary of the Army, Ryan McCarthy, mobilized the DC National Guard to keep the protestors away from our national monuments. The threat was self-evident; the night before, a wave of agitators had demolished the temporary fencing erected to protect the White House, national monuments, and other sacred spaces.

The rioters made their way to the White House, with violence, looting, and injuries left in their wake and seeking to foment a direct assault on the executive branch of our constitutional Republic.

But it wasn't just DC. That night President Trump tweeted, "The National Guard has been released in Minneapolis to do the job that the Democrat Mayor couldn't do. Should have been used 2 days ago & there would not have been damage & Police Headquarters would not have been taken over & ruined. Great job by the National Guard. No Games!"

Secretary of the Army Ryan McCarthy immediately ordered the DC National Guard to provide additional barriers and a cordon to the northern perimeter of Lafayette Park to the south at Constitutional Avenue NW.

Meanwhile, more protestors gathered to what had now become an

Antifa staging area north of the White House outside Lafayette Park. To those of us who had experienced combat in the Middle East and around the world, what we were witnessing had the makings of a pre-assault gathering of troops. The DC Guard had not been exposed to such domestic violence in decades.

On May 31, after multiple violent clashes with protestors and rioters, resulting in numerous injuries, the DC police, National Park Police, and National Guard troops were able to stop this initiative, causing a brief stand-down of the protestors. BLM and their comrades in Antifa, with this avenue defended, then turned their attention to St. John's Episcopal Church, just outside the park. St John's Episcopal Church was not only sacred to those who worship there, but also famous as the sanctuary of President Abraham Lincoln, who during the dark days of the Civil War would arrive every night and prostrate himself before God in brokenhearted prayers for a nation torn asunder by the sin of slavery.

Yet they chose this special place to set ablaze in the demonstrations over the death of George Floyd. They burned the parish's Ashburton House basement and set other fires in the church itself. They sprayed graffiti on the worship space of President Lincoln, the one man who led the United States to unashamedly proclaim that *all* men (regardless of their skin color) were equal in the eyes of God and the government. Ignorant to the nature of the famous Washington, DC, landmark church that had once served as the forge for the Gettysburg Address and Lincoln's Second Inaugural Address, protestors scrawled words of grievance: "I can't breathe" and "George Floyd" and "ACAB" (All Cops Are Bastards).

Few understood the irony. Even (moron) Charlie Dupree, rector of St. Paul's Episcopal Church, was nonplussed by the damage to the sacred space. He told a local ABC News affiliate that he didn't want to clean the church. Rather, the rector of the church that was a national symbol for every sitting president since James Madison wanted to keep the graffiti as a reminder of the change that was needed. It is a testimony to the politicized moment that the rector of a church burned by a mob would then support the mob and ignore the disrespect of those who would attack both the White House and the church in their pursuit of what they call social justice. Again, it was Trump, after all. Dupree went on about the graffiti, "I consider these memorials. They represent those people who have lost their lives to injustice." The pastor folded, but thankfully St John's had a racially integrated and professionally trained military, police, and fire department to protect the church and extinguish the fire.

* * *

The night I arrived at the armory, the national media was breathlessly covering the possibility that President Trump would utilize the Insurrection Act to deploy active-duty military into American cities. While Washington, DC, which does not hold the status of an independent state in the union, would still be under the jurisdiction of the federal government and could have federalized troops occupy and protect the capital, this is not true of the fifty states that make up our union. With nary a constitutional crisis or the need for a presidential usurpation of constitutional authority, the 82nd Airborne would show up days later to help reclaim order and stability in the nation's capital.

The media, of course, ignored the threats to the White House, the president, and the national monuments that were under attack. Armies of armed and violent left-wing extremists were trying to deface and destroy the White House. They beat the crap out of Secret Service agents. They wanted their hands on Trump. With any other president, and at any other moment, the Left would have compared this day to September 11, just like they did with January 6.

Instead, the media-driven collective memory of the moment was President Trump famously displaying the Bible in front of the burned church after the clearing of Lafayette Park. If Trump is with us, then everyone else is justified in being against us. Take that to the bank from the Left—both inside and outside the government.

The context of the president's demonstration at St. John's, blurred by a media that ignored and minimized the threat of public disorder, was to show the nation that he would not allow the mob to dictate security around the White House. He had just won a battle for the security of the nation's capital in opposition to the woke mob, the mayor of DC, and most Democrat elected officials. "LAW AND ORDER" he tweeted in defiance.

Not only was he facing the mob and Democrat politicians; he was up against his own Pentagon. General Mark Milley appeared briefly with President Trump in Lafayette Square on June 1, 2020. He claims he didn't know cameras were there, and claims he left as soon as he found out, later telling the media that it was a "mistake." Not only is Milley an idiot, but he's an arrogant ass who just wants to be liked by his fellow Democrats. Only someone with no regard for the rank and file, and an obsession with the perception of the DC bubble, would say something so absurd.

Milley thinks that standing with Trump for a few minutes, outside the White House, and showing strength is a mistake so huge he has to beg the media's forgiveness. Milley quickly apologized for appearing with the commander in chief, catering to the chattering class of other partisan generals and of course the media. He even considered resigning in 2020, according to a *New Yorker* article in 2022. He drafted a resignation letter that—unsurprisingly—he never had the courage to deliver. In the letter he basically called Trump a fascist and a racist. But, instead of having the courage to resign, Milley decided to keep his job and "resist" Trump under the guise of defending democracy. At the inauguration on January 20, 2021, Milley is said to have told former first lady Michelle Obama, "No one has a bigger smile today than I do." A partisan to the end, dutifully advancing the priorities of Democrats—even when they're not in office.

* * *

As my mini deployment in DC grew from hours to days, so did the crowd surrounding us, growing to thousands of people. At night there were three times the number of protestors in the street. I had no command. I wasn't in charge of anything or anyone. I was just another officer in the DC National Guard and tonight I was going to be just another infantryman standing in a line with the American military who had been dispatched to bring peace to the streets of Washington, DC.

"You that guy from FOX News, sir? *FOX & Friends* on TV," a young, enlisted soldier asked me.

After years of being recognized on the streets, I have grown accustomed to this line of questioning. Normally I would smile and offer to take a picture. In my Operational Combat Pattern (OCP) uniform, in the midst of blocking protectors and adjusting the face shield on my Kevlar helmet, I had to separate that from the mission at hand.

Without making eye contact I said, "Not today. Like you, I'm just a soldier."

"My mom and dad love you."

"Thanks, buddy. Stay safe." I smiled warmly and turned toward him, powerless to resist a mom-and-dad shout-out.

My gear was on and now, side by side with my brothers in arms, we moved forward to a previously unforeseen battlespace. America. Our own soil.

The noise grew louder as we approached the line of soldiers and police. We paused briefly inside Lafayette Park, where the damage from the night before was evident. Scorched earth, scorched buildings, graffiti everywhere.

The other side is playing for keeps, and not by the rules.

We quickly became aware of the waves of rioters who gathered their strength and threw themselves at the soldiers in the front lines. Shields held high, our lines held up against the repetitive force of their attacks. Like twenty-first-century hoplites, the soldiers formed shield walls and did what they could to hold their ground against an aggressive and manic adversary. Every so often a frozen water bottle, or a loud plastic thud, could be heard from a soldier blocking something meant to crush their bones.

This was chaos. My mind reeled as I tried to process anything similar to what we were experiencing. Was it like a soccer riot? Or a marketplace in a third-world country? While the similarities to foreign combat entered my mind, I could not react how I would as an American soldier in a third-world nation. These were not locals in Baghdad protesting an evening curfew. These were not disaffected opium farmers saber rattling outside Marjah. These are America's sons and daughters. My fellow citizens (mostly). Co-laborers in the grand experiment of our constitutional Republic. No matter what happens, no matter what they do, they must be respected and not harmed—unless we have to defend life or limb.

Looking around I see the fear and anxiousness in the eyes of National Guard troops that have held their ground. In all ways they are superior in skill and strength, but they have no endgame, no kinetic ambition, or ability to end this chaos. There was no doubt that we could win this battle. Easily. This was not a fear born out of cowardice. Nor was it a panic that emerged due to failed leadership. This was the acknowledged danger of intentional and definitive restraint. Heroic and decent restraint.

(On the foreign battlefield, we made fun of this concept—written by armchair generals in air-conditioned offices. In America, it was a reality.) The other side—our fellow citizens—set the terms; we defended.

This was patriotism in action and on display for the world to see. Most of us wanted to fight back. Within ten minutes, I became one of them. As your muscles ache and your eyes fill with sweat and dust, you begin to seek closure with a sense of resolve. We could easily have pushed this line back, snatched the leaders or the loudest protestors in Antifa, and sucked them back behind the lines. If this engagement were to occur in Samarra or Kandahar, we would be home by breakfast.

This was America. And no one wanted to take a fellow citizens' life. These DC Guard soldiers were short-staffed, which was why I was now just a guy with a shield in the ranks taking orders like a private. They were resilient and fundamentally decent citizens of the nation. They were getting pushed back tonight just like the night before when they ended up with their backs to the fence of the White House. The only difference in the conflict was that on this night a new fence was behind us. Taller. Stronger and reinforced with concrete Jersey barriers.

Dear Lord. Just like in Iraq.

During the day the police and National Guard took all that ground back they lost the night before. From the back of this hot summer crowd, a quiet lull began to reverberate over the masses. The protestors from the front disengaged our line and made their way for a new company-sized element of angry protestors.

Something is going down.

I was here because the call went out within the unit that all soldiers with combat experience were needed. And like a kid saying hello to me for their mom and dad, that was also something I was powerless to resist.

I am needed. I gotta be there.

Although my job in the DC Guard was in a headquarters unit, this was going to be different. A group of us got together on the Armory floor—NCOs and officers—and agreed we were all in this together. My battle buddy, as it happens, was black. Thought *nothing* of it at the time, but the other side made it pertinent. Wherever we were needed, we would go. Tonight, we were needed. We grabbed shields, visors, and a baton and stood with our fellow soldiers.

A frothing protestor with a ski mask approached a black soldier to my right.

"House n——. You Uncle Tom, betraying motherfucker. You sell out your people like this. Come over here. Come to this side. You coward n——."

The Black Lives Matter protestors approached the line to walk it, identifying their targets of opportunity. They knew sticks and stones would cause us to break their bones—but words could fly freely. We were not instigators; we were a defensive force. So here came the taunting and vile racist oratory—targeted at black soldiers, and black soldiers only.

"Your country hates you."

"Why would you wear that uniform in a country that enslaved your ancestors and treats you like a second-class citizen and would throw you in the trash at any moment?"

"Y'all see all these other white soldier boys here? They like those Confederates. They like General Lee. They run things. They're in control. They don't like you. But you're fucking useful, Uncle Tom."

"You're a traitor to your ancestors who were enslaved by the white man. And now here you are."

"You call yourself a man, but you're hiding behind a shield and camouflage for a country that hates you."

As I looked around at the black National Guard soldiers dealing with the stress of the moment, the protestors' words started to penetrate. It was unrelenting. It was sheer racism. And the good guys were on the verge of snapping.

One female soldier was being screamed at from a distance that would make even detractors of the CDC's COVID guidance blush. It reminded me of Billy Martin, the famously bellicose manager of the New York Yankees, screaming at a baseball umpire before being thrown out. The spittle was flying along with the invective. Country. Racism. Supporting the patriarchy. How dare she serve as a black woman. To my right, it was directed to a black male soldier. I saw the soldier's face register at what was being said like, "Yeah, what *am* I doing here?"

Both participants across the line are the same age. They are both products of the same educational system as those screaming on the other side of the line. The only difference was they made a different choice about what they serve.

* * *

The Guard unit I served on that day was integrated, it was loyal, it was effective, and it showed a restraint noticeably absent from politicians and protestors. We did our best to do minimal harm to our fellow citizens on the other side of the line. We did not batter them physically, nor did we attempt to undermine them mentally or emotionally. We simply held the line. Our opponent showed no such restraint.

Tears began to build in some of the black soldiers' eyes. A swarm of agitators gathered around those black soldiers. The racists smelled weakness. They ignored all other soldiers. They screamed at them like some BLM version of *Scared Straight*, the old-school TV program where convicts would attack young wayward youths to get them to turn their lives around. I haven't seen this coordinated level of verbal abuse in my lifetime. It was unrelenting. Far worse than the most malevolent fictional sergeant in basic training. These soldiers showed their character and worth. They stood tall and stared straight ahead. Furling their brow and pursing their lips at some of the cruelest, hate-filled attacks I have ever heard.

One soldier, who could take no more, broke rank and was immediately replaced by another. She collapsed in tears and was gathered into the arms of another soldier who heard the disgusting remarks she endured moments before, offering comfort—mental first aid—as if that soldier had been pierced by a round.

I could overhear from behind me a leader consoling one of the black soldiers. "Fuck those guys. You're serving your country. You're serving your community. I need you in this. You are my family now. You and me. We are going home. I got you. You got me."

My head was swimming. Trying to show a stoic but vigilant posture. Looking around for any soldiers that might break. And any soldiers looking ready to retaliate. Oddly it was the white soldiers who were starting to show the twitch of combat readiness. Their instincts to protect their teammates began to remind me of the stories told about Dodgers shortstop Pee Wee Reese, who often led the charge against the racist taunts directed toward his teammate Jackie Robinson. Jackie famously knew he shouldn't retaliate against the racist barbs of his opponents, but nothing precluded Pee Wee from taking a swing.

I personally witnessed a black soldier who, while being ridiculed by a protestor, looked over to another white soldier who had become unnerved while watching the entire thing and said in a measured tone, "Stand fast. This is what they want us to do. Hold your position and keep your cool. Now."

I could immediately tell this was an NCO giving that order. He was cool. He was calm. And he was in control of his emotions. Others?

It was impossible to expect that level of discipline from the lower enlisted and noncombat arms soldiers. Some had only left their hometown to go to college or Army training. None had deployed to combat. The combat vets had a totally different posture than those that were not. Those hardened men and women who had seen war, they were ready for anything.

While staring and scanning ahead, I spotted the first shadow in my periphery. Then they began to rain down upon us. Red construction bricks. Soldiers from the back gave overhead cover with their riot shields. These guys did not learn this in the DC National Guard. They were combat veterans. The Romans had a shield formation they called the "tortoise." They placed their shields over the forward formations to give overhead cover and the flanks. Nothing could penetrate this formation. Even arrows fired down would not injure those in the "tortoise." We use the term "lock shields" today to show a sense of loyalty and endearment of a friend sticking by your side through thick and thin. Channeling our inner hoplite, we formed an ad hoc barrier against projectiles that was as effective as our shields allowed.

A hail of objects rained down. Too many for every plastic shield to deflect, the bricks and debris impacted a few helmets and rattled many cages. One brick flew at a soldier to my left. The shield hit his face . . . hard. His lip spit red before he was able to register that he was hurt. His verbiage was John Fetterman confusing. Others started to panic at his injury. They assumed that their brother had suffered a brain injury. He had not. Just a bruised and busted-up face.

Lucky him.

I wanted to calm lots of soldiers down and tell them it was going to be okay, but I had barely spoken at all since I arrived. Stoic silence felt like a more productive posture. I am not leading anyone out here. I am not in charge; I am just following orders, and in control of my actions.

The injured guardsman quickly backed out of the line to the medics and was immediately replaced.

I looked over to some of the more experienced veterans. This was our time to get serious. No more standing here and taking bricks to the face. We needed to set a tone. The mood in the crowd had changed and now they were no longer a nuisance; they had become a gathering threat. Someone was going to get seriously hurt. Screaming at soldiers was one thing; using the crowd for concealment and pitching red construction bricks into our faces from fifteen feet away, that was another.

"Get in line," someone boomed from the back.

Another injured guardsman fell somewhere in my periphery. I heard movement and assumed both were replaced. One particular sweaty Antifa guy on the other side wouldn't break my line of sight. If need be, I would pop this guy and keep him down. The voices of those who were screaming and shouting began to fade into the background. I could still hear what the other black soldiers were being told as protestors screamed unconscionable things in their face.

I was shocked back to full volume as our riot visors, already dripping with spit and sweat, now streamed with yet another, now foreign, liquid. Whatever it was brought great joy to the crowd. I could smell the acrid smell as another amber-filled water bottle burst right in front of me.

Urine.

My last experience with piss bottles was fifteen years ago, when I had to keep my soldiers in towers at Guantanamo Bay from leaving them behind. There were no bathroom breaks at 2 a.m. in a watchtower, so they did what they had to do. Now Americans—that same age—were throwing them at us.

This was like a prison break.

While the riots lasted for weeks, it is important to remember that those who served as first responders in Washington and across the nation were the overwhelming victims of violence. They rarely retaliated, and almost never instigated. That is what I witnessed before me on that domestic deployment. While their fellow citizens on the other side of the line cast aspersions on their life choices and loyalties, the men and women of the Guard and DC law enforcement, regardless of their race, faith, or orientation, acted with dignity and professionalism.

The only sin these black soldiers had committed that night was to serve their nation in uniform and protect our national institutions from defacement. Not a single guardsman had moved on the protestors. No one had unnecessarily touched a single protestor at that point. Yet they were the enemy; not because of who they were, but because of their allegiance to law, order, and the Constitution.

The reason those men held the line with such honor and discipline was all the things about them that the Left hated. They were normal, strong men with honor. Guys who refused to let what made them different distract from their unity and brotherhood with other soldiers. Men who put others first, and didn't try to be the center of attention. Men who refused to see themselves as victims. You can't resist those sorts of taunts unless you have a rock-solid sense of self—and they got that, in large part, from the American military.

We held the line and were composed again. We were very aware that any overreach by our forces or police would look like we were targeting protestors. Everything was being filmed. By professionals and amateurs.

At that moment, I had an epiphany. The Antifa and Black Lives Matter rioters were not any different than our soldiers. In fact, we were quite similar. We were passionate. We were brave. We did not fear pain or what the other side could do to us. We believed in the righteousness of our cause. At any other time in American history these protestors would have fought injustice by . . . joining the military. Today, we are on separate sides.

Why aren't these kids fighting for justice in a uniform with a flag on their shoulders? This is literally the exact same pool of people that all my soldiers in Gitmo, Iraq, and Afghanistan came from. The same neighborhoods. The same emotional framework. The exact same public schools. What changed between 1999 and 2020?

The other side—Antifa and BLM—trained and worked together. They had discipline and a plan. They executed their plan. They were proud and courageous in confronting us, as they would have been fighting Russia, China, or ISIS.

How could America have eroded so badly that we are standing off against our own citizens? Cameras pointed everywhere, yet the message was not being sent. There was no way this could have gotten this bad without someone in our government knowing about it. All of these young potential soldiers had found a terrible form of heroism—either because they'd rejected the good kind or, just as likely, because our government wasn't confident enough in our goodness to present it to them.

As I held the line that day, I realized that anything could happen, and my gut told me that none of it was inevitable.

Chapter 8

SUPPORTING DEI MEANS SOLDIERS DIE

Black Americans have never missed an American war in uniform. At the time of the Revolution against Britain, it is estimated that approximately five thousand black soldiers served under George Washington and his generals. In those days, there were plenty of simple jobs on the front line, but few colonists had the esteem or level of specialized skills needed to serve in the artillery. So it's telling that many black soldiers served in the Colonial Artillery, an illustration of their professionalism and ambition. General George Washington promised freedom to any black soldiers who served—and over one thousand received that freedom. From second-class citizens to free men.

Just a few years later, in the War of 1812, General Andrew Jackson promised the same freedom to enslaved blacks, particularly in the Battle of New Orleans. He lied. He betrayed his honor and turned his back on the black soldiers who had sacrificed under his command. The treatment of minority soldiers, like the treatment of all soldiers, was contingent on the morality of the military and civilian leadership in charge at the time. Rights are not rights when they are contingent on the favor of government or political leaders.

Black Americans have too often had to fight for equal treatment in institutions that persisted in highlighting—to use a lefty term—their "otherness." What's ironic is that after centuries spent working toward equal treatment, these same institutions have reversed that victory to resegregate service members by individual characteristics. Today, the new race essentialists—calling themselves "anti-racists" and wielding "Diversity, Equity, and Inclusion" (DEI) programs—want nonwhite Americans more "othered" than ever! Our military is, intentionally, going backward.

The core source of the problem lies in the military knuckling under to the personal whims of civilian leaders, yet again. Ask any white or black soldier in formation today—guys who serve together and deployed together—and 99 percent will tell you that racism is *not* a problem in today's formations. But we're being told by activists and politicians *outside* the military that racism is rampant and must be addressed. As such, our military leaders are hunting for a problem that doesn't exist. Even a quick look at the history of black American soldiers shows that it's only by resisting such personality-driven fads that we can achieve justice for all.

Black Americans died and bled with equal courage and valor well before they were treated equally under the law. Just look at the Buffalo Soldiers, the Harlem Hellfighters, and the Tuskegee Airmen. Every time Americans fell in battle, black soldiers sacrificed alongside every other American soldier. But it was over 170 years of sacrifice before Harry Truman signed Executive Order 9981 in July 1948, finally integrating the United States military.

To the twenty-first-century ear, it seems impossible that it took so long for Americans—and their government—to acknowledge the fundamental equality of all citizens within its borders. We are aghast when we learn that freedom and citizenship were withheld from friends and neighbors. The truth is, however, that most countries are slow to put to rest long-standing racial or tribalist hatreds, if they do it at all.

America's prejudices over the centuries have been sinful, but America is not unique in its historical racial and ethnic biases. These problems have existed around the world and continue to exist in many of the places where American troops serve globally. What is unique in American history is our success in navigating the fundamental flaws of human behavior and tribal identity structures.

The most intransigent bigotry I have seen was outside American borders. When I served in Iraq and Afghanistan, I sat for months listening to tribal Sunni leaders tell me how different and suspect their Shia neighbors were. People who lived a kilometer away were hopelessly separate and distinctly problematic. They bickered about how strange the other sides were. They wanted to *kill* them, and often did. Educated in the American understanding of racial equality and the military ethos of multiracial brothers in combat, I came home understanding how backward these people were on topics of ethnicity. Sure, America had its history—and is far from perfect—but we look like utopia compared to *real* racism and intractable hatred.

At the time we asked the question of how we could help them recognize the error of their ways and open their minds so that they would not want to kill their Muslim neighbors. It was a hopeless exercise. You can't be a great civilization if you intentionally limit a distinct portion of your population from being a part of your national greatness. Hence, they are not.

* * *

131

Yet here we are today, resegregating our military yet again. In the name of weeding out any hints of racism (mostly fabricated) and to force so-called inclusion, the American military has become race-, sex-, and "extremism"-obsessed. The push for military diversity has moved beyond the traditional goals of equality of opportunity and into the realm of racially, sexually, and politically based outcomes. We have resegregated ourselves, one box check and one PowerPoint presentation at a time.

In an organization where "good order and discipline" are maintained by adherence to standards and commitment to mission success, anything that undermines the meritocracy of competence wounds the effectiveness of the war machine. First it erodes it, then it destroys it.

That is what Diversity, Equity, and Inclusion (DEI) initiatives have done to the American military. DEI amplifies differences, creates grievances, and excludes anyone who won't bow down to the cultural Marxist revolution ripping through the Pentagon. Forget DEI . . . the acronym should be DIE or IED. It will kill our military worse than any IED ever could.

In both world wars, white soldiers did not receive awards based on their race; they received them based on their service and actions. The crisis of the past was that black soldiers in those wars did not get awards because of their race. They were denied valor awards because they were black.

Today, we have flipped the script. The American military is recruiting, promoting, and giving awards to soldiers on the basis of settling an undefined DEI score, using a sliding scale of racial, sexual, and political preferences. We are told we can right the wrongs of the past by perpetuating an equal wrong in the present. The historically "oppressed" are now *always* preferred over the historical "oppressors"—even though these categories meet *very few* of anyone's lived realities, especially while in camouflage. It's black over white. Female over male. Gay over straight. And, with Obama and Biden in charge, certain political persuasions are "extremists."

It's social justice reparations in camouflage.

Guilt for the sins of the past are guiding the policy of our future. Worse, that guilt is being leveraged by ideological extremists to advance control over the military. When I think about my career in uniform, in almost every instance where there has been poor leadership or people in positions they're not qualified for, it was based on either the reality or the perception of a "diversity hire." I could tell you stories but will spare the guilty the unnecessary shame; all were good men, they just were not qualified leaders. Elevating an unqualified person into leadership will never increase the effectiveness of a team or a unit. It will only increase the chances of your team being unprepared for the challenges that you will face—or erode the authority of a leader who deserves to be there but is seen as a "diversity hire."

In an office environment, this dynamic means certain people lose out on opportunities. You risk lowering morale and maybe a chance at a quarterly profit.

At war, this policy gets soldiers killed. Morale plummets and the mission suffers. Everyone loses—and some lose their lives.

Americans expect that opportunities be equally afforded to all races, creeds, and genders—that is the standard. And no one wants the scales to be weighed against anyone's success. Only the most racist passenger would be offended to discover that his pilot is black, but no passenger would be happy to know that their pilot was flying their plane because of a program that allowed lesser qualified individuals into the pilot's chair in the name of "inclusion."

The fundamental danger of a woke military is not that there are no grievances to be addressed. The danger is that they are addressed capriciously and by fiat through regulations and political machinations. The difference between the promises made to black American warriors by General Washington and Andrew Jackson was that they were promises made by a person, not covenantal expectations carved into the law. Promises made by people or parties can be retracted as easily as they can be offered. Just ask those African American soldiers who were betrayed by Old Hickory.

In a piece for FOX News, journalist Michael Lee interviewed anonymous soldiers about the new woke military initiatives. What he was told was revealing and is yet another reason why the Army is missing its recruiting numbers every year.

One anonymous soldier told Lee, "I 100% believe the military is woke. I see, daily, minorities, overweight people, and women not adhering to military standards."

Another said. "Nobody corrects them due to the fear of being fired and labeled a racist or a sexist."

When asked about the new "woke" Army, Biden's secretary of the Army, Christine Wormuth, stated flatly in a 2022 press conference, "we get criticized, frankly, sometimes for being 'woke,' I'm not sure what 'woke' means."

She paused and moments later, almost thinking aloud, added, "But, first of all, if 'woke' means we are not focused on warfighting, we are not focused on readiness, that doesn't reflect what I see at installations all around the country or overseas when I go and visit."

Yet, minutes later, Secretary Wormuth contradicted her previous statement by adding, "I do think we do have a wide range of soldiers in our Army, and we've got to make them all feel included . . . that's why a lot of our diversity, equity and inclusion programs are important."

So training, lethality, discipline, and readiness are in fact secondary to people having a diverse buddy sit with them as they share their Chili Mac MRE? We have a secretary of the Army who thinks her branch of service is a DEI summer camp with bad haircuts. Even though it's not ideal, *civilian* organizations can afford to treat their people like a successful kindergarten, where everyone's differences and feelings are catered to. But the military cannot afford it. The military isn't about celebrating differences or emotions—it's about celebrating commonalities and forging discipline. It's an institution that makes and requires adults (normal people) who can think beyond their individual needs to the betterment of the group.

New woke ideology undermines this by obsessing over divisive history and victimhood. Former secretary of state Mike Pompeo—a West Point graduate—wrote, "How can we ask young men and women who have decided to risk their lives for America, even die for America, to affirm that our country is inherently racist? How can we ask them to view their brothers and sisters in arms through the narrow prisms of race or gender? The clear and obvious answer is that we cannot—not without putting their lives at risk on the battlefield. A woke military is a weak military. Unfortunately, woke and weak are exactly what our military is becoming under Biden's leadership."

Joining a team often starts with self-interest, but if that continues to be your priority, you have a problem. Ultimately, your main question should be, simply put, how are you making the organization better? Every company, every team, every partner wants someone who is adding to the mission, adding to the success of the team. The primary reason the Left enforces these woke policies on the military is to take *full* advantage of the culture of following orders from leadership. Soldiers have no choice, so you weaponize the honor and duty-bound fidelity of the enlisted to not question lawful orders, and woke bureaucrats eagerly adopt nonsense policies they stole from the human resources department at National Public Radio.

So-called diversity is not our strength; it is our weakness. Unity has always been the strength of our military, and anybody with a brain in their head knows it. Yet here I am, having to argue with these idiots. The scary reality of our moment is not how the military went woke and weak, but how our leaders allowed it to get that way. We are led by small generals and feeble officers without the courage to realize that, in the name of woke buzzwords, they are destroying our military. Standards are being flushed down the toilet, followed quickly by readiness. And then American lives.

My concern is that the woke military no longer shares the basic mission that has always directed us toward our true north. The mission of the woke military is not to be better, faster, and more lethal; it's to be more diverse and inclusive so that we feel better about ourselves. This is bullshit, and it's not worth serving for. This social-justice-obsessed generation anticipates the Memorial Day where they can hold their heads up high at the dynamically diverse burials at Arlington National Cemetery, without realizing that what is more important is the discipline, competence, and lethality of the warrior who goes home after the fight. We went from giving the enemy no comfort and no quarter to having designated hugging stations to embrace each graduate at the Air Force Academy.

Furthermore, the woke military is changing the default settings of racial behaviors and attitudes. The woke military currently assumes that if you're white, you harbor racist views. You can't not be racist; you need to read about being an antiracist. This is perpetuated by a complex system that benefits from keeping the bifurcation of racial identity something that we fight over.

While the woke military continues to see the nation as if it were populated by a generation of Jim Crow–era southern sheriffs, I would posit that my generation is about as close as we have come to achieving Dr. Martin Luther King Jr.'s dream. My parents taught me there are racist people in this nation. They would hammer that "we are *not* those racist people. Some people may think *these racist* things, that will never be tolerated in our house. That is not what we believe in our home, that is not how you operate in this family." My neighbors said the same.

When I played sports like basketball or joined the military, I was surrounded by people of all classes, all races, all backgrounds—and in a meritocracy like sports or the Army, none of that matters. Great teams want the best people in the best places. Diverting our behavior away from honoring merit in choosing starters, leaders, or advancement is the most disruptive force to communities, teams, and organizations. It's like a basketball team where the coach's kid starts but is clearly no good. When you disrupt the natural course of a successful team by forcing upon it rules that resist the full opportunities for each person, you fight against the natural inclination for people to rise to their natural level of giftedness and injure the effectiveness of your organization.

Sports are a lesson—you pull your starters when you are dominating the opponent to show sportsmanship or play the chubby kid to give him a lesson in life—but combat is real life. *My sniper had better know how to fucking shoot.* My artillery needs to be 200 meters from my face to impact this enemy bunker. I am sorry daddy didn't tuck you into bed and let you know you are coolest kid in the neighborhood, but we got Chinese communists to kill before they run us over. I fully understand military service is not for all people. I very much noticed the absence of the loudest voices screaming in Washington, DC, about DEI in shithole places like Samarra, Gitmo, Afghanistan, and during the racial tension of 2020. If you don't feel good about yourself, and don't want to join the military, you are free to do something else.

But you do not have the right to exploit the decency of our warriors and use them as a petri dish for your social engineering experiments. Our soldiers are subjects—daily, unit by unit—in these twisted woke diversity experiments and it's gutting the very fabric of our fighting force. Just ask someone serving. They will tell you. That's why parents don't trust the military with their children. Our allies don't believe we will honor our word. And our enemies no longer fear us.

Under Joe Biden, the world has never been more insecure. And our military has never been so fractured, weak, and bereft of cohesion.

If you are going to start global wars with your policies—like in Ukraine or Taiwan—at least allow the warrior class to pick the teams they need to clean up your mess. We choose talent. We choose discipline. We choose merit.

This is the military. This is war.

We enter the twenty-first century with the military mimicking the Marxist universities in how they operate. While American academic strength has sunk to the levels of a third-world nation, with minority high school graduation rates under 50 percent in many of our largest urban areas, the military thinks it should take a lesson from the university system that has victimized generations of minority students since the halcyon days of the 1960s.

Why would any sane person look to our failing university system, with rampant grade inflation, a horrific record of stealing the future wealth of the young, and escalating evidence of dangerous indoctrination on their own campuses, and proclaim that the military needs to take lessons from these false prophets?

Can anyone with an ounce of objectivity proclaim that the national experiment on progressive campuses has created a more decent and tolerant society? Ironically, as the university system has become more concerned with a command-and-control ideology, the military has been infiltrated not just by liberals who desire a less draconian military, but by little totalitarians who are demanding compliance with university-style edicts in social programming.

"Oh, my pronouns. I use those in the university. Now I get to use them in the military too!"

"No more 'yes sir' or 'no sir' [as the Marine Corps recommended to their drill sergeants in 2022]. We are all gender-neutral now!"

And it all becomes part of the pipeline. "Oh, my Pentagon emails got pronouns just like the university." As I'm writing this, the Pentagon just removed all gendered language from award citations. Soldiers no longer "distinguished *himself* or *herself* in battle" . . . they distinguished *themself.* Even my Word document tried to autocorrect that word. It's not even real English, but it is stupid and self-defeating.

Political progressives have infected the Pentagon, starting with Clinton, then to Obama, then to Biden, pushing outside cultural priorities that are way beyond integrating the military into a social justice, politically correct view of the world. The big theme of their agenda is the wanton and intentional destruction of meritocracy. In a world of "equity"—a communist word—meritocracy is evil, unfair, and always racist. The Pentagon must be brought to heel, one solider at a time.

In combat, if you master the art of war, your reward is—to live. And you cannot survive combat if you don't surround yourself with merit-based skilled professionals in the most critical positions. Combat requires survival. Survival comes from courage and excellence, leadership, training, and readiness. All of that combines with your chance to survive—by closing with, and destroying, the enemy.

Not a single thing that's being pushed through the Biden administration is attempting to improve any of those things. We are not more lethal; we are more likely to lose. That's it. Bottom line. We will lose future wars, just like we are losing recruits. Soldiers who endure Pentagon briefings about nonexistent, but somehow rampant, racism—retire. Soldiers who get passed over for promotion because a certain race must fill a certain slot—retire. Leaders who refuse to go along with the woke nonsense—retire or get pushed out. Civilians on the outside who see what's going on—choose not to join. Worst of all, military leaders who go along with the leftist social experiments—get promoted. It's been that way since Obama, and is on hyperspeed today.

Chapter 9

MEN NEED PURPOSE, NOT INCLUSION

March 2006
FOB Brassfield-Mora
Samarra, Iraq

I couldn't concentrate. And I desperately needed to focus. Sifting through information handed over by Iraqi informants at Forward Operating Base (FOB) Brassfield-Mora—in a side room of a dusty makeshift operations center—the only noise was the displeasure of my computer's hard drive stubbornly motoring through all this dust, only interrupted by my own yawns reminding me that my overtired body needed rest. This wasn't cram-for-finals tired. This was nothing like running suicides in an empty gym for Coach Gunderson because "I pushed the ball, and didn't flick it." This was sleep-deprivation-induced nausea.

I was tired when I led a platoon on a midnight air assault mission a few months ago. I was spent on those endless overwatch missions when we watched the sun rise twice before we called it a patrol. But back then, my soldiers looking to me for our next move focused my mind to complete the mission. The communal shame of being "that lieutenant" who was too soft for his tough infantrymen was something I would not allow myself to experience. My rifle clacking off my gear . . . my sweaty Nomex gloved hands adjusting maps . . . empty Rip-It cans cracking in my cargo pockets . . . the radio squawking over my shoulder . . . all helped, back then, to interrupt any prolonged internal soliloquy that could be used as temptation to quit. This was always mental. And the consequences were life and death. Then I had a forged team. A platoon of infantrymen. Two months ago, I would collapse into my Conex bunk after hours of patrols as 2nd Platoon leader, or Chopinn 26 on the radio. The flaccid canvas on my boots would stand at attention from the hardened muck, sweat, and filth.

Here, in that quiet room, I am basically alone. An Army of one. Never truly alone, but it was late.

And I can't. Stop. Yawning.

The year was 2006 in the restive area outside of Samarra, Iraq, nestled in the heart of the Sunni Triangle just due east of the mighty Tigris River. Less than eighty miles to the south sits Baghdad, the grand central station of mujahideen recruitment and supply.

For some reason, this new job—Assistant S5 at Battalion—left my eyes pulsing with exhaustion each endless day. The job was "Civil Military Operations," which basically means building relationships with local tribal power brokers. Along with my direct report—Captain Chris Brawley, an amazingly capable and affable soldier—we made up the job as we went along, forging local relationships, building human intel networks, keeping people alive, and arranging dirt naps for many more. If I hadn't trusted my immediate chain of command—most especially a phenomenal executive officer, Major Steven Delvaux—I would have thought our little outfit was being set up for failure. After three long and bloody years of violence, this region and her agitators were poised for more. This was the slowest of moving freight trains, as intelligence was pointing to Samarra being one of the next stops.

One more pass. Am I missing anything? Focus. Stop drifting and focus.

I worked in "civil affairs" during the beginning of the sectarian-fueled civil war in Iraq. Doing civil affairs work in Samarra in 2006 was the equivalent of opening a Union flag store in Charleston, South Carolina, a month after Fort Sumter. Less than thirty days ago, Al Qaeda in Iraq destroyed the revered Golden Dome in Samarra in a complex and rehearsed command detonation. With it, they obliterated any chance of avoiding a full-blown civil war in the country. Samarra was no longer the backwater of the terribly named "War on Terror." Now the destroyed Golden Dome was the recruiting poster for Iranian loyalists, Shia militias, government forces, and Abu Musab al Zarqawi, who was slowly taking Al Qaeda away from the influence of Osama bin Laden.

Things that would have dominated my life at home were now the routines of a stranger. At any other time in my stateside life, these spartan conditions, this vacant sterile office, the hectic pace would be damn near my personal rock bottom. As that image finished processing, I realized that I had crossed the line. I wasn't a basketball player getting a Princeton degree. I wasn't another Ivy League grad making fistloads in finance. I wasn't even a Wall Street Princeton grad playing Army. I was a combat veteran doing my generation's part in war.

I was an American Soldier.

This wasn't the bottom. It was the top.

Some of the names on these informant lists I reviewed would turn out to be "High Value Targets"—but only after an exhausting amount of research. *Who are these guys? Which Muhammad is this? Why this tribe? How can we be sure?* I am sure some S5 officers didn't take this job as seriously as we did—if you wanted to phone in the job, you could. Power-Point presentations could tell a neat story, but real intelligence, real relationships, and real results come only from taking real risks. Most S5 officers are not out to prove they belong in the fight—I guess I just felt obliged. If my former platoon was still kicking in doors, the least I could do is help empower more good guys and kill more bad guys.

Life lesson: your motivations are totally different if you know what it's like outside your air-conditioned office. Mine certainly were. One of the Left's biggest problems is thinking that everyone's greatest desire is to be "included." For some people, it is. But for most men—especially the military type—it is much more important to be *purposeful* than to be safe or included.

"It is impossible to understand what's going on with American men without paying attention to the world they inhabit," wrote author Samuel James recently. "It is a world where meaningless work is governed by soulless human resources departments. It is a world where most men live increasingly automated lives, unable and then unwilling to use their hands.... The emerging American man possesses nothing, creates nothing, for nobody in particular."

Leaving that world was transformative for me. I was a part of the fabled 101st Airborne Division and I came to this group of seasoned warriors not from West Point or a Midwest recruiting station, but from a perfectly good job on Wall Street. A capable, trained Soldier sitting on the thirty-eighth floor of a Manhattan skyscraper analyzing IPOs was not going to cut it for me—the chance to serve my nation in a real shooting war was impossible to resist. Leaving the world of comfy financial analysis—and volunteering for combat in a controversial war—confused my new platoon as much as it did my family and friends. My fancy-pants Princeton degree wasn't exactly a welcomed data point to infantrymen either. They didn't care, nor should they, that I had been an underdog my entire life. Those traits don't jump off résumés, nor can they be relayed on hour-long phone calls with a branch manager in the now-renamed Fort Benning, Georgia—as I groveled and maneuvered to be put into the action.

In 1999, my senior year in high school, no one recruited me to play NCAA Division 1 basketball. There was lukewarm interest at best. In fact, no one really cared if I showed up for opening practices at Princeton my freshman year. Sure, the coaches coldly included me, but I was not welcomed; making the Tigers varsity team was uncertain at best. I was not in their plans. But I persisted. I worked my ass off. I arrived early, stayed late, and never took days off. I had to prove myself. Proving that I belonged on the court—somewhere—was a huge part of my evolution into adulthood as a young man. My dad and I sent dozens of VHS video highlight tapes along with typewritten letters to every major basketball program that was dumb enough to publish their address. Let's just say the response was . . . underwhelming.

No one wants you.

I wasn't "included" just because someone wanted to meet a quota. That was a good thing. In many ways, that experience prepared me for being the new kid in the "Rakkasan" chow hall—the storied 187th Infantry Regiment of 101st Airborne Division. The moment I stepped behind my new formation at Fort Campbell, reality came crashing down around me: I was way out of my comfort zone and way over my skis. In retrospect, it didn't help that I showed up wearing an outdated Army National Guard uniform that no one on active duty had worn for over a year. I didn't even have time to order the new Army Combat Uniform (ACU) that was approved for service use in 2005.

Awkward.

Being the new platoon leader of an infantry platoon before a looming combat deployment was like meeting your arranged marriage bride at the altar. Joining the 101st just to go to combat required a transition from the comfortable cushioned seat I held as an equity capital market analyst at Bear Stearns. Not the most common path to combat with an infantry platoon and turned out to be the most difficult thing I have ever done in my life. Like the videotapes sent to college coaches, my persistence paid off. I knew one guy: the captain who trained me to be an infantry officer. He needed a combat platoon leader. He got his boss—the famed Colonel Michael Steele—to agree. I got my National Guard unit to release me. And, eventually, my barrage of emails and marathon phone calls with faceless Pentagon decision makers got me slotted into the combat platoon leader slot—just in time to ship out. The day my orders were approved, a colonel from the Pentagon called me, and put it bluntly: "Your orders to 3-187 are approved. I don't know who the hell you think you are, or how you did this, but *don't fuck it up!*" Mission accomplished. Now I just had to endure the deserved sobriquets of *Wall Street*, *Princeton*, and *National Garbage*.

The pile of paper was blocking the flickering screen of my outdated Army computer. The local informants—naming more and more names—came in waves like ballot returns on election night. It was overwhelming at times. Those names didn't sit in my green Army notebook, and then my inbox, for very long. The Samarra City Council president—with his networks of sheikhs, tribal leaders, and miscreants—would gather intelligence, then offload it to me, almost always in person. At first it was a few names; then, once they saw our efficacy, the floodgates opened. Then it was up to our small team to verify, vet, and advance the information to those who would prosecute justice on the guilty—and sometimes we did it ourselves. That adjudication process usually took a day or two, but sometimes mere hours. A name, address, and phone number would be called in or handed over—we would run it against our existing HVT list—and like John Wick, that name was bleeding on the floor of an Al

Qaeda safe house sometimes before I went to bed. Or I woke up to the beautiful news.

The clock was ticking, and we were wasting time.

The bad guys moved fast. Changing phone numbers, addresses, locations with maximum paranoia. My primary job was to make inroads with local tribal leadership, but the intelligence they gave us was more valuable. They had to know we were stakeholders in their own security. That we listened and trusted them. Only then could we expect reciprocity. A safer Samarra made everyone's lives better. For me, it meant saving American lives. Every terrorist we didn't have to leave the gate to pacify was a victory. Some nights it was too easy. The name would literally match up with known terrorists. The locals simply gave us information as to what foreigner was living among the locals. Iraq and the greater Middle East aren't exactly known for having a robust Department of Motor Vehicles, meaning most times an ID photo was outdated. A name was common. We needed more information. Cell phones. Car identifiers. Eyewitness accounts of last known whereabouts. I left Wall Street to chase down bad guys with a rifle . . . and ended up joining *CSI: Samarra*.

By March 2006, with less than sixty days logged into this dusty computer, over two dozen of these missions have led to direct kills of known insurgents. Many more captured. It was an incredibly edifying feeling, being part of a team that was killing and dismantling Al Qaeda—at least in our area. Pushing through my exhaustion, I remember thinking to myself: *this is why I traded out high-paying Wall Street . . . to hunt down Wahhabis.*

Our 3rd Brigade commander was Colonel Michael Steele, most known for his leadership of the 3rd of the 75th Ranger Regiment in Mogadishu, Somalia, back in October 1993—a battle etched in cinematic lore as *Black Hawk Down*. There were few battles of the modern era that would make soldiers fanboy more than that epic urban battle in Somalia. Colonel Steele was surely aware of his reputation preceding him with his subordinates, but he never let on to it. He never talked about Somalia, but it forged his zeal for killing bad guys. He didn't care what people thought of him, only what Zarqawi thought of his leadership skills—resulting in piles of dead enemy combatants. Steele would not have lasted a day on Wall Street. All his takeovers were hostile. He was a warrior, and he demanded the same focus and seriousness of his entire unit. Our commander was in the Sunni Triangle to win each and every day, there was no room in the 101st Airborne, 3-187 Rakkasans for anything less than total dominance of the enemy. That was the expectation that we all understood. It was all man, all merit, all mission. There was no room for nonsense, or bullshit, or excuses.

My body was bone-weary and my mind melting down, and I felt a scratch in my throat. I was so tired that all I could do was grind my teeth, just like when I jumped in a full-body ice bath after another three-and-a-half-hour Princeton basketball practice—almost all of which was defense, like a dutiful second teamer. This was a new type of exhaustion. When you get tired, you make mistakes, and that truth was as effective as cold water in my face—keeping me zeroed in on the task at hand.

This mission was my life. I thought daily: if I could have my family over here, I wouldn't leave. *Ever.* You always miss family, but the men I served with were my new meaning and purpose. Two years ago, almost to the day, I had deployed to Guantanamo Bay, Cuba, with the New Jersey National Guard's 42nd Infantry Division. Those guys were family, but that was a cute camping trip compared to this. This was war. Everything I had ever done in my life led me to this moment. I was living off adrenaline and passion, despite the stress that made me feel as if my internal organs had been removed and replaced.

Euphoric stress.

Glorious exhaustion.

Each "storyboard" (an Army PowerPoint slide that summarized missions with maps, evidence, killed/captured, etc.) that confirmed that our little S5 team was providing intel that led to kills of bad guys built my confidence like I was back in high school draining three-pointers against our rival, Mounds View High School. After the first couple of informant leads led to bad guys at room temperature, I felt like we had found the right team. After a dozen more, I knew I was good at this. *Our team was good at this.* Relationships lead to trust, trust leads to intel, intel leads to dead bad guys. *Rinse and repeat.* After twenty-five, I realized that perhaps my planetary purpose was to proactively, politically, and then militarily destroy Islamist radicals. *Feeding a well-oiled killing machine, now that's my jam.* My talents were appreciated. The hard lessons I learned as a new platoon leader in the unit were not done (solely) to embarrass me or put me in my place as the FNG (fucking new guy)—but more importantly to forge me, quickly, into a member of our team. Our tribe. A warrior.

Muscle memory kicked in every time we met with another tribal leader or pored over a map of the city with AK-wielding, chain-smoking (temporary) allies. We would analyze the human terrain, pick the right targets, grab the informants, and then either act on it ourselves (with the help of eager and willing infantry platoons) or pass it along to John Wick. Everything else faded to nothingness. As a dedicated Minnesota Twins fan, I couldn't tell you anything about their starting rotation or early season potential to win the pennant that year; something I loved to do when I was a civilian. Baseball is baseball, but this was the big leagues.

I was focused on what insurgents were coming to town, and which had fled. Where were their new safe havens? What neighborhoods did they control? What tribes were in bed with Al Qaeda? Working with us? *Both?* All information had to be triple-checked—without tipping off the locals about what we knew, and what we were planning. The entire job was subterfuge. Our friends were treated with respect and caution. Our enemies were treated with respect and violence. Some days you found out the difference only after you'd spent an entire night raiding house after house after house. Colonel Steele made it clear—our op tempo was up all day, open all night, sleep when you must.

Nothing was easy. No simplicity in this battlespace. The bad guys could just be local boys who insulted another local leader's daughters. Or some midlevel sheikh who insulted the clout of a tribal elder. Nothing was taken as fully true, until the puzzles were solved—and sometimes, they weren't. Even then, we couldn't always know. But here's what I did know: the United States Army's heralded 101st Airborne Division could not be used to exercise petty, personal assassinations just to curry favor with local leaders.

The radio chatter down the hall frequently startled me back into my work. Radio updates brought in a cacophony of chaotic background noise that reshuffled the deck in my brain—usually at a time I need to both focus and sleep. Sometimes it was mundane patrol check-ins, sometimes troops in contact, other times: John Wick got another.

Never time for celebration, only on to the next informant, the next tribal meeting, the next night of raids. But each time with more swagger and confidence. Planning the next operation, I looked at this morning's early mission and moved that file to the other pile. That's another one. Colonel Steele was a machine, the infantry line units indefatigable.

As I wrapped up another after-action "storyboard" report, I looked over a map and cross-referenced the statements and descriptions of the insurgent and his tribal affiliations. Without looking I slammed back a bitterly stale mouthful of coffee out of a dirty Styrofoam Cup O' Noodles container. I didn't even know what time it was, let alone the day of the week. I was confused as to the last time I saw the news or took a shower. We reset once a week, on Sunday morning, when we played a game of stickball in the back corner of the FOB for forty-five minutes—rifles stacked nearby.

There was nothing left of the old Pete Hegseth. I was part of something bigger and better. I was only one soldier, but our team was powerful. At that moment, I would never allow myself to be tired again—at least not here. My body never again registered the privations of my service as a burden or a sacrifice. I was not collecting stories to share with my grandchildren one day around a glowing fire. This was my purpose. I reveled that I was strong enough to endure deprivations to complete the mission. In that moment, I rewired my brain to see every struggle as the dedication of my soul to the outcome. The comforts and conditions of home life became an ever-fading, detached memory. As if I was reincarnated from a past life.

I distinctly remember swelling with motivation as a Grinch-sized smile uncurled across my face. I saw my dusty reflection on the computer screen. Young. Motivated. Half-shaved. Making a difference. I was needed. I had no idea what tomorrow would bring, but I was ready for whatever challenge would be presented. It was well past 0300 hours. In the frantic work of the day, my today had become tomorrow.

* * *

The military doesn't always make men good—anything can go sideways. But most of the things feminists hate about men, labeling them "toxic masculinity," are really just men that are undisciplined. Men that are chaotic, confused, and aimless. Want more confusion? Let your schools go woke. Want more chaos? Let your cities go woke. Want more so-called toxic masculinity? Let your military go woke. Because, while America may run on Dunkin, our military runs on masculinity, properly channeled. It's not toxic at all, it's necessary. Just because the rest of our culture has gone soft, and effeminate, and apologetic—doesn't mean our military can afford to. Staying tough, manly, and unapologetically lethal is the lifeblood of the fighting man.

Of course, masculine men can be "toxic"—mistreating women, disobeying orders, or harboring racist views have no part of military masculinity. Those aspects, and others, cannot be tolerated. And they have not been tolerated in the military for decades. But those are the outliers—and we've allowed the Left to define all masculinity as toxic. And by targeting the ethos of the military, the Left is ensuring more truly toxic masculinity in the culture. Don't let the military forge honorable masculinity; then you will get unchanneled, rudderless masculinity in the civilian world.

Men don't want to be included; they want to be purposeful. They want to be *needed*. That is what I felt on a remote base in Iraq and while training troops in Afghanistan. It forged me.

A woke military, on the other hand, doesn't speak to or forge such men.

On the front end, a woke military emphasizes the made-up military values of "diversity and inclusion" and fails to recruit the masculine men who make up our warrior class. This is self-evident. My high school, in mostly rural Minnesota, produced some great warriors—tough-as-nails, masculine football-playing studs who were looking for their next masculine pursuit. One of my friends joined the Marines, another the Army Rangers—later wounded and decorated in battle. They were masculine high school boys, who—at that time—saw the patriotic, tough, masculine messaging of Marine Corps and Army advertisements and said, "Hell yeah, I want to do that." In both of their cases, the military forged raw, possibly "toxic" masculine man, and created trained, disciplined, honorable masculine men. Who knows what the untrained and unconstrained world would have made of these alpha males, but the military made great warriors—and now great citizens.

A woke military also fails to recruit the not-so-masculine men who, after proper discipline and training, become the masculine men our military needs. Or young men who don't come from military families, but love the country. In some ways, I fall into this category. I wanted to "be all that I can be." I also think of two other high school friends. Neither played sports; neither was particularly tough or "cool." But they came from good, patriotic, Christian families and went to basic training after high school. Call it duty, or a challenge—but they stepped up. One of those men just retired after twenty years as one of the Air Force's top jump-masters. The other is still a lieutenant colonel in the Air Force. They went from weak and timid to tough and disciplined. A "woke" military probably would have recruited neither of them.

On the back end, a woke military doesn't actually discipline the troops it has—breeding a culture of fake, or toxic, masculinity that is anathema to a highly functioning fighting force. You get one of two things from this. First, either disenchanted troops who thought they were joining a tough meritocracy but instead are met with a social justice alphabet soup. They mock the institutions they join and get out early. Or you get troops who play the "game" just to get along, and are never fully formed by the traditional military lifestyle. They "get used to" the woke military, never actually learn how to maintain discipline and standards inside their units, and the military gets less disciplined. You end up with people-pleaser careerists instead of decisive and noble leaders. In both scenarios, our military gets weaker.

Chapter 10

MORE LETHALITY, LESS LAWYERS

December 9, 2005
East Al Rashid
South Baghdad, Iraq

The wash of the rotor blades taking my platoon on a raid was deafening. I counted nine soldiers in my chalk as we lifted off, three other UH 60s on our tail heading toward the target—all full with Charlie Company's 2nd Platoon.

I slapped my gear to assure myself that I had everything I needed. This had long become an irrational fear. Getting to the objective and not having an essential item became my standing-naked-in-front-of-the-class nightmare. (To this day, I have regular dreams about combat missions where I cannot find my rifle.) Radio traffic blared in both ears like I was running a 911 dispatch center. Company net, platoon comms, and internal pilot conversations interrupted my thoughts.

My GPS was in my leader pouch, my maps in my cargo pocket, my magazines ready. Brass to the grass. Fresh batteries for my night vision and PEQ2 laser aimpoint.

You have everything you need. Just stop it. This is going to be fine. Everything is fine. Just . . . breathe.

I had overplanned. There was nothing I was going to see tonight that would be a surprise. This was my best asset. My platoon was going after the bad guys, and I would be ready. I adjusted my helmet-mounted radio microphone, resting just over my chin strap.

"LT," my Charlie Company First Sergeant Eric Geressy squawked in my ear. He was going with us on this mission, something he did not have to do. Geressy would go on to earn a Silver Star (should be a DSC, but that's a story for another day!) on his next deployment in Iraq. If you entered a laboratory to design the prototypical, badass infantryman, it would be Eric Geressy.

"Choppin 7, this is Choppin 26," I responded by the book.

"Let's go get 'em, National Garbage," he said. Bringing a smile to my face.

"Roger that, Choppin 7. National Garbage out." We were headed out to hunt Al Qaeda tonight.

* * *

Four months ago that was meant to break me down. Make me wish I was back on Wall Street. Now it is a reminder of how far we have come, and how much I've been embraced.

Back at Fort Campbell, a new platoon leader from Princeton, coming from a job on Wall Street, I—as you know—arrived at the unit out of uniform. My platoon sergeant squared me away quickly, personally taking me to CIF (Army supply)—I don't even know what it stands for, I just know it's where you get all your shit.

A few weeks after arriving at Fort Campbell, we were in Kuwait. Living in giant tents, and fine-tuning our training. My first assignment was the assignment nobody wanted: company equipment layout and accountability. Normally this was the executive officer's (XO) job to handle at the company level, but they often outsource it. So he made sure I got it. The clipboard was handed to me as if this was the equivalent of taking out the garbage. Reading serial numbers in the hot sun. Confirming serial numbers in the hot sun. Writing confirmed serial numbers on the clipboard in the hot sun. Rinse and repeat, all in the hot sun.

It was a shit assignment that every officer hates. But at that moment, I loved it. I was where I wanted to be. I'd rather count every rifle, every radio, and every "sensitive item" in the company one hundred times before I sat my ass on the thirty-eighth floor of Bear Stearns in New York City and crunched numbers on an Excel spreadsheet for boring meetings with really rich bankers.

"Hey, National Garbage, after this layout make sure the fucking radios get filled." First Sergeant Geressy studied me with a squint in his eyes.

The 101st Airborne is one of the most storied divisions in the military. My National Guard time logged was not the least bit impressive to them. They all heard my origin story by now and figured that I was some John Kerry wannabe. A check-the-box, entitled rich kid. On the surface that is exactly how it appeared.

Soon enough, I would face a challenge that would call on all my training and preparation. The rubber was about to meet the road, and the messiness and chaos of modern combat were about to become crystal clear to me. So much of today's media conversations about warfare

are from the perspective of people who have no idea what it's like in a firefight. They're armchair generals, drone aficionados, or micromanaging dilettantes. What I was heading into would forever teach me respect for our soldiers doing impossible jobs in impossible conditions. Video games are definitely *not* combat—nothing clean, clear, or easy about it.

Those days in Kuwait I had an inkling. But it was still in my future. That's why 1SG Geressy was sizing me up. He understood that visceral feeling of leading men in battle. He knew that I had never led men when the bullets broke the sound barrier over your shoulder, sounding like the finale of a Fourth of July fireworks display. He knew I didn't know what it felt like to experience the slim difference between a near miss and a knock on your parents' door from a notification team. He didn't trust me. But did I trust myself? Everything else falls into place when you know who you are and what you are capable of. But, at that point, I still wasn't quite sure—a quiet confidence couldn't shake the disquiet of the unknown ahead.

This was my job now. And we're headed to combat. This wasn't Guantanamo Bay, where I had been deployed the year previous. And I wasn't in New York. There was nothing life-or-death about New York. Sinatra famously sang—in "New York, New York": If you can make it here, you can make it anywhere. He was full of shit. Subways replaced by Humvees, briefcases with body armor, and the white noise buzz of air-conditioning replaced with the rotors of helicopters. The smacking of a coworker eating his lunch at his desk exchanged for a M240B machine gun eating belt-fed rounds as the red tracers spit up dirt downrange.

One day while training stateside another lieutenant from Charlie Company took me aside and said, "They are going to come at you. They will come at you and figure out who you are. Just let your competence speak for itself, or at least show that you are listening to your NCOs. You will make people believe you are ready when we go downrange."

Over and over, I told myself:

Don't stop training. We're going to do more training. We're going to train every one of these guys on more medical combat lifesaver, more react-to-contact drills, more trigger time. I want the guys to do another rotation through the shoot house. With night vision. And white light. More and more. I need more, so I don't let these guys down.

I chose to be here. I practically begged to be here. I'd made the bureaucratic drug deal of the century to get here. No menial task would make me quit or stand down. I loved it all. Throw more retard-level clipboard tasks at me, and I'll keep throwing them right back at you—performing novice-level tasks with the anal-retentive dedication of a paranoid Princeton graduate.

When we arrived in Iraq, someone would inevitably ask me, "Hegseth, you played basketball at Princeton for Coach John Thompson, right?"

"Yes, I did."

"You guys ran the Princeton offense, right? Did you play in the Big Dance—the NCAA Tournament?"

"Yes, we did."

No one wanted 1LT Hegseth playing Division 1 basketball either. Every day I showed up, a low-level recruit from nowhere Minnesota, determined to outshoot, outhustle, and outwork anyone. On the junior varsity team, I hovered for two long years. Earning Coach Thompson's trust was a Herculean task. My goal was to make not playing me tough, or at least ignoring me impossible. It took eighty points across two JV games my sophomore year to get an eyebrow raised. Never giving up in practice and playing defense against the starting five—for hours and hours—made me dependable. Never quitting and planning out the opponent's reaction to our game plan during coaching sessions made me invaluable to the team.

By my senior year, Coach Thompson would stroll over to the bench during an opening moment in the game. Without taking his view from the court, he would ask, "What do you see, Hegseth?"

"Their zone is soft along the baseline. If we can rotate the ball and get it there, we'll get people open cutting to the middle when they have to guard the baseline. And from there, we can pop the ball out for open threes."

Coach Thompson finally broke his gaze off the court to smile at me with a nod of his head. It took years to gain the trust of the son of coaching royalty—and a damn good coach in his own right. Didn't hurt that I was a son of a high school basketball coach. And wouldn't you know that when the defense was stretched, they broke down, and our open shooting guard drained a three.

I belonged here, even if nobody ever seemed to fully appreciate it.

* * *

Exhaust and whirling rotors hypnotize me into another place far away from here. I have to break myself out of it when I hear the crew chief animatedly get my attention.

"Two minutes, sir. Two minutes to LZ," he cracked over the internal headset of my bird.

Thirty-six hours ago, I got word our platoon had been selected for this mission. When I got the Warning Order (WARNO), I was walking on air. Exhilaration that we would be doing something meaningful and kinetic. Pulling every satellite map I could find from the TOC (Tactical Operations Center), I pored over the contours, the target reference points (TRP), the phase lines, the features that I could easily recognize if the worst-case scenario occurred.

Two weeks earlier, my platoon sat in ramshackle guard towers, wasting away in the heat and dust. Aimlessly spitting tobacco juice and sunflower seeds into Halliburton Hesco barriers at the front gate playing "Fuck, Marry, Kill" with the cast of *Friends*. Everyone was frustrated by how we were being used by our battalion and brigade. *I just spent a year guarding terrorists at Guantanamo Bay, how in the world did this unit end up on that same duty in Iraq?* When missions started coming into the S3 (our operations shop) for high-value target raids, the entire Charlie Company chain of command screamed, "We're here, we've got the assets. Use us, please."

In 2005, much of Baghdad was run by the Army National Guard. Our area of operation, FOB Falcon in the East Rashid neighborhood of the city, was also patrolled by a National Guard unit. They were taking heavy losses. The unit's battalion commander was killed by a roadside bomb; he was killed while responding to the death of one of his company commanders. It was bad. That year 844 Americans would lose their lives, half of them coming from improvised explosive devices (IEDs). Baghdad was a meat grinder.

I was changing my radio battery in the main TOC when I heard those deaths called in. These guys were facing a buzz saw every day—and you could see it on their faces every time they rolled through one of our gates. There was nothing we could do for them; it wasn't our battlespace. We were only allowed to overwatch the two hundred meters outside the perimeter of our FOB, and maintain base security. We left the wire to find mortar and rocket teams and clear out adjacent buildings. That was it.

At night, units started to notice a string of gruesome street killings, mostly sectarian in nature. However, with the insurgency starting to boil up, these discoveries were all under the surface. Streets, patrolled all day, would be littered with civilian bodies by the middle of the night. Hands tied. Close-ranged handgun wounds to the side or back of the head. Women, men, even children. Units that saw no visible sign of enemy contact would routinely roll up six to ten dead bodies on the street. They appeared out of nowhere. Killed in another area of Baghdad. East Rashid was just the dumping ground for the day's kill.

Finally, with the battlespace getting more and more dangerous by the day, our company's lobbying for action proved successful. My 2nd Platoon was tasked for a "kill/capture" mission. An Al Qaeda terror cell—mortarmen—had been wreaking havoc in the area. Our job was to catch them by surprise in the middle of the night and kill or capture them.

Speaking of "kill or capture," the rules of engagement in Iraq in 2005 were complicated, confusing, and sometimes upside down. Different units had different policies, even though there was supposed to be one, uniform standard. Different unit missions, different leadership ethos, different areas of operation, and different enemy tactics equals lots of confusion. So upon arrival in Iraq, we were briefed by a judge advocate general (JAG)—an Army lawyer—regarding the latest "in theater" rules of engagement. Needless to say, no infantrymen like Army lawyers—which is why JAG officers are often not so affectionately known as "jag-offs." There are some good ones out there, but most spend more time prosecuting our troops than they do putting away bad guys. It's easier to get promoted that way.

Near the end of this particular jagoff's talk, he used the example of an identified enemy holding a rocket-propelled grenade (RPG):

"Do you shoot at him?" The JAG officer stood in front of my platoon with his arms folded.

And my guys were like, "Hell, yeah, we light him up."

"Wrong answer, men. You are not authorized to fire at that man, until that RPG becomes a threat. It must be pointed at you with the intent to fire. That makes it a legal and proper engagement."

We sat in silence, stunned.

After this briefing I pulled my platoon together, huddling amid their confusion to tell them, "I will not allow that nonsense to filter into your brains. Men, if you see an enemy who you believe is a threat, you engage and destroy the threat. That's a bullshit rule that's going to get people killed. And I will have your back—just like our commander. We are coming home, the enemy will not. That's our view. We're not going to kick down doors and just start shooting people, but we're going to be aggressive."

As I've shared, Colonel Michael Steele was our brigade commander—and he was a certified badass. He suffered no fools. If you engaged the enemy and destroyed it under his command, you got a "kill coin." Colonel Steele would have been a horrible gender studies professor at the University of California, but there was nobody you wanted more in a combat situation. Because of his tenacity and leadership under fire, many boys and girls are being raised by their veteran fathers, instead of visiting their graves.

* * *

The fastest two minutes of my life sped by as I felt the Black Hawk skids rest down onto the ground of our landing area. The voice of the pilot was a bit uneasy, but I didn't know any better. Something felt a bit off. That was the smoothest touchdown I have ever experienced in a UH-60. We didn't pop or bounce down. We sunk. Like an Oreo in milk. Just plopped down.

Nine members of my platoon poured out of the UH-60 under the heavy wash of the Black Hawk rotors. I could see the other three roar down near me. I instantly felt the cold temperature. It was December in Iraq—warm during the day, but the desert heat gives way to chilly nights. The temperature drop had a bite to it because all of our senses were up.

I started looking around as the platoon piled out of the last UH 60 and the birds were immediately outbound. At first it was roaring loud, and with every passing second the scene got quieter and quieter. Then, silent. Only the soft sound of small movements. I'll never forget that moment of quiet; it's still where my mind goes today when I'm outside, at night, in the quiet.

As the men take a knee and begin to scan targets, I pull out my GPS with the waypoints preprogrammed. I see the green screen of death. The GPS was nonoperational. I turn it on and then off.

No way this is happening. Come on. Come on.

We are in Indian country—no-man's-land, controlled by the enemy—*and my equipment decides to shit the bed!?* I checked the batteries twice, I know they're good.

Without hesitation I pop back to my hours poring over the terrain on my cot at FOB Falcon. Looking up I see the minaret of the mosque to the northwest. I identified that as one of my "oh shit reference points." I compare that spot with the bearing on my compass. I look at my map.

Okay, we need to get five hundred meters to the east of that wall.

Nothing was easy in Iraq. And this night was just getting started. It's nearly pitch black—although a partial moon aided our night-vision goggles—and we are going to use nothing but terrain features to get to the target house.

Since this was our first mission, the company leadership team, the Charlie Company commander and first sergeant, were right beside me. Everyone assured me that this was *my* mission to run. My entire chain of command was present, but I was leading this assault. I knew the details.

I knew the maps. And, as such, I felt the pressure of the moment weigh on me. I did my best to beat my own monstrous expectations down and focus on the mission.

My boots sank three inches into the thick muck of a farmer's field before I realized that we were at least half a kilometer from where we were supposed to be dropped. *Those damn pilots dropped us in the wrong spot!* Add that to the five hundred meters I was already rerouting, based on the terrain I had memorized, and I knew that this mission was already off to a rough start.

In every Hollywood movie there is a slow-motion shot of the heroes stepping off the bird and moving toward the objective. The astronauts walking slowly to the rocket ship. The cowboys slowly moving toward vengeance. I had long envisioned my platoon's moment in a similar manner, but after I gave the order to space out and move by squad formation in a modified wedge, every guy's boots lodged in the vacuum-like suck of the Iraqi farmer's plowed muck. Taking extreme effort to lift and plant, soldiers began toppling over, the clank of link ammunition rattled, the clatter of weapon systems and gear smashing. Soldiers were dropping one after another in this mud field of manure and overirrigated soil.

D-Day plus three minutes and it was already a cluster. We were briefed that the terrain in our LZ was hardball solid. Instead, we got dropped in mud.

The squad leaders moved their fire teams to cover and I spotted a dirt road that would get us moving in the right direction. I was *pretty sure* we were moving in the right direction. I decided to box, or avoid, the dangerous open areas and to skirt the main roads, to make up time. We were farther away than we had planned, and needed to make up time. We didn't have time to beat brush. Speed could preserve our element of surprise, so speed would be our security.

The soldiers moved, following my guidance. There was no hesitation. It was the most special moment I'd ever experienced. Looking at these men. Strong. Tough. From Nowhereville, America, just like me. My men. They all look different. Different races, and different dialects. But all normal dudes. They're all individuals—but not tonight. In the here and now, when a crack of a Dragunov sniper rifle could end anyone's life at any moment, we are one. No excuses, no medications, no women—just men. Men trained to fight. Men tough as nails. Men, with no distractions.

I knew exactly what they could do. They earned this place, their ranks and their positions. We snaked along the country road like we trained for. One hundred percent commitment. One hundred percent in it for each other. If Lucifer himself were on the other side of the street, these thirty-seven men would have run headlong into the fire for each other.

The old Army infantry adage is "slow is smooth, smooth is fast." And this has been gospel to many infantry units for generations of battle. However, fast is also fast and I made the assessment that our best security would be to speed onto the objective. The men dashed across intersections, each time holding ground to pull security for the next soldier to pass.

The morning we got the WARNO telling us to be on standby for this mission, I immediately started studying the satellite intelligence imagery and vehicle movement signatures that had pegged the hide house for this rocket team that was launching 107mm Soviet-made rockets in and around Baghdad. I studied everything around that house, and the surrounding houses. I knew the neighborhood better than my neighborhood in New York.

In Iraq, the 107mm rocket was akin to the Katyusha rocket of the Soviet era. It was normally fired off the back of a flatbed truck. If unidentified, the truck could fire and quickly speed off. If tracked, they were fish in a barrel to be taken out from above. Our mission was to kill or capture the rocket team. We were expecting four to six bad guys in this cell. It consisted of an older, gray-haired cell leader and possibly three to four younger mortarmen.

Thirty minutes into the movement, my platoon found itself in the backyard of a house about fifty meters from our target house. We were already ten minutes behind where I thought we would be at this point. I heard a dog barking on the other side of the wall where two of my squads awaited my next order. My element was split in half, with one section of the platoon in the courtyard of the house next to our target and the other on another piece of property. Then another dog reported back.

Within a half minute, a few neighborhood canines were ralphing out danger with bellowing, baritone yelps. The Iraqi version of ADT had just been tripped. The lights at a nearby house lit up, and we could hear brush ruffling. The time in the hourglass was pouring fast in my head.

For the first time in months, Wall Street seemed like a good gig.

This was decision time.

Using hand and arm signals, we quickly informed the adjacent squads to form a hasty wedge. Whispering into the radio, I told the back element to form a file to follow directly behind the leading formation's wedge. We were going to send a two-squad infantry arrow formation into our target compound. Three to five meters of separation between each soldier, with clear and open firing lanes to their left and right, we would move quickly. The other two squads were overwatching the objective from an adjacent vantage point. The lead wedge would establish security and hold that security to cover the file that would go immediately to the back door of the target house (we assessed early on that this was the best entrance). Each job transferred over to the next guy without saying a word. Training, trust, muscle memory. This was instinct to our unit.

If we made contact before we entered the target home, all soldiers would react to any enemy fire. They would lay down suppression fire and assault, or envelop, the enemy's base of support. A leader in combat isn't giving instruction to each piece of the team. We give formations and plays. Soldiers make the decisions as to how best to maneuver. My job was to be in a position to best coordinate battle movements, and in this mission I felt I needed to be near the front of the formation to make the right calls.

Six short months ago, I thought pitch meetings were stressful.

The hope was to gain ground with time to spare, breach the entry, establish security, and gain a foothold. If three to five insurgents presented a threat, our spacing and automatic fire would cut them down or immediately suppress them to a hasty cover. Although this was not exactly my original plan, which gave me some pause, I liked these odds.

Just go with it.

I keyed my radio and whispered into my headset mic, "First and Second Squads, this is 26. Target house, eleven o'clock. Fifteen meters. On me. Go. Go. Go."

As it happens, as the men moved, I found myself as the third man in the stack on the initial entry into the house. It is not ideal, nor Field Manual desired, for a platoon leader to be in a stack entering and clearing an insurgent layer. Statistically it's not usually the first man in the stack who receives hostile direct fire during a breach in a close quarter battle. The number two man gets hit most of the time and the number three man about 10 percent of the time. That will just have to be the roulette spin for tonight.

We kicked the door open and the teams overlapped responsibilities exactly as we had trained. It went flawlessly and I took great pride at how quickly they dominated the building's first floor. The men moved quickly from night vision to white light.

We found children. We found women. We caught them still sleeping, only fully awakened after our lights danced on their bodies.

We quickly established that there were no military-age males in the home. But many did live here.

I noticed some of my veteran soldiers—who had done a previous tour—talking. I was leading this assault, but they had valuable insight. I listened to First Sergeant Geressy as he approached me calmly.

"Whatcha thinking, LT," First Sergeant asked.

Coach Thompson would stroll over to the bench during a tense moment in the game. Without taking his view from the court, he would ask, "What do you see, Hegseth?"

"First Sergeant, dry hole. Nobody's here. We're searching for everything. Three hours from the sun coming up. What do we do? All we found was this ammo box. Nothing they aren't allowed to have."

"No way, LT Hegseth. You did well. See that little green ammo box the boys brought you by the stairs." First Sergeant Geressy pointed with a helmet nod.

An NCO ran over to pick it up from a table and brought it back over to us to further examine with white light. That foreign writing turned out to be Chinese.

"That's called a Type 63 scope. Used primarily for . . ."

"—a 107mm rocket launcher. The Iranians use these for the Haseb rockets too," an NCO on his second tour finished the first sergeant's answer.

The determination in my first sergeant's eyes matched mine. He trusted me. After all the tests, he and the company commander, Dan Hart, gave my platoon this mission and trusted me to lead it. And now he was fully invested with his soldiers to finish the mission.

"We got ourselves exactly what we came here to get. Now we just need to find them."

"What do you suggest," I asked him.

"I am asking you, LT." First Sergeant looked into my eyes.

This is it. You earned this moment. Think. Breathe. You belong here.

"I am not sure that gun sight would be effective if they are hitting built-up areas."

"Now you are thinking, LT."

"So this guy is either stupid or maybe just . . ."

"Maybe just a guy who keeps gear because it's cool? And doesn't realize Americans are smart and this just gave away his operation." First Sergeant knew all these answers already.

"This isn't the cell leader. No way."

First Sergeant Geressy smiled at my realization. I earned his respect and now together we were planning. In a fight, rank was merely ceremonial. Leaders are leaders, regardless of pay grade or age. Experience and integrity are far more important.

"This guy, the guy who lives here is just a punk. Who fills tubes and fires shots." First sergeant was teaching me as he was thinking out loud. Realizing he had a student listening to every word he uttered he continued methodically.

"Which means, we can squeeze this dude. And he will talk."

"We just have to find him. He is probably long gone, right?" I asked first sergeant.

"He will be as long as he thinks we are," first sergeant said as he moved the curtain from the front window. Looking out of the house, he turned to me. From there he sped up his tempo of conversation. School time was over. First sergeant was in execution mode.

"We take one squad, plus three men. Back to exfil. Black Hawks take them back to the FOB. Send all four birds to pick them up. Sir,

ALL FOUR BIRDS COME TO LAND. Few get inside. Make it loud. Make it obvious. Make it stupid. This is the entire point. The rest of your platoon, automatic riflemen preferably, stay right here with you and me." He smiled assumingly.

I looked over the men. This would be like cutting players on your team. They all trained hard and wanted this as badly as anyone. Finally, I decided on one squad. The rest stayed behind. The UH-60s would be inbound as soon as I radioed to the TOC. The plan was underway.

One squad left, making lots of noise as they did so. Lots of spacing, looking like a larger element. As they did, we turned off all the lights in the house and the courtyard. Soon after, the loud noise of Black Hawks overtook the area. Roughly ten soldiers got on board, spacing out into all four Black Hawks. The PZ (pickup zone) was different from our original LZ (landing zone) so the enemy likely did not have surveillance on that location.

With the noise of outbound Black Hawks in the background, the lights out, and the house silent, we set up a kill zone. With automatic weapons overlapping fields of fire with the front driveway and down the road. Concealed, ready. And there we waited. We kept our medic in a room with food and water with all the women and children. All cell phones were confiscated. Safe, quiet, and all in one area of the home. The house was dark, no lights on.

From the soldiers who had deployed before, we knew that military-aged males often slept in different houses—or fled to a safe house at the sound of any aircraft, drones, or troops. We also knew that, after coalition forces raided enemy-held terrain, their occupants usually returned home the moment the coast was clear. This was cited time and time again by other veterans of Iraq and Afghanistan. The dogs always returned to their vomit to smell around.

Humvees are loud. Bradley Fighting Vehicles make some disturbing noise. Nothing compares to the roar of one Black Hawk helicopter. Four send a message.

America has left the neighborhood.

We waited, in darkness.

Just under an hour later, two men strolled up the driveway, looking around for any signs of Americans in hiding.

This was like Publishers Clearing House dropping off a big carboard check at our front door. For an hour we were watching . . . and then the adrenaline immediately spiked. I was excited. This was the type of moment I had wanted. A yearlong deployment to Guantanamo Bay promised some action. But it was minimal, mostly watching Al Qaeda terrorists playing soccer and eating sandwiches. All we wanted was to take part of the kinetic action that made a difference. This was my first time out on mission leading an element. And these two fools walking into the house made my heart pump out of my interceptor ballistic vest.

Our guys were good, and the two insurgents were unarmed. As they approached the door, soldiers swarmed them from all sides. We threw them down, threw on zip ties, and whisked them into the house. No lights. No loud noises. If more were coming, we didn't want to tip them off.

The edifying nature of watching these arrogant thugs just walking toward the driveway, thinking they were good to go, and the looks on their faces when a squad of boys from Tennessee and Kentucky popped out was a life-changing moment for me.

'Merica, fuck yeah.

Two more times that night—about twenty minutes apart—two men strolled down the driveway. They got the same treatment. Bagged, gagged, searched, processed. None of them had any idea we were still there. We got in our licks but had a larger objective in mind.

A couple of the names and identification matched our target lists. Now we needed them to sing. First Sergeant Geressy earned all the rope and latitude he demanded. He did some "on-site interrogation" and one of the men tossed up a name and address down the road. We knew these two were both low men on the chain and the bigger fish was out there.

Quickly, it was revealed that our "big man" was the old man down the road. He was the cell leader. That turned the night around. We were in the bonus round and these points were double. But the sun was about to come up, and the neighborhood would soon know that "the Americans" were still here.

Working on the actionable intelligence from a very startled mortarman in custody, we put together an ad hoc group that moved tactically down the road, raided the house, and found the older male cell leader. He came out of the house, acting like a local farmer. He smiled and thanked us for keeping him safe. Our interpreter was wise to the ruse. That's all I needed to hear, and we took him down immediately.

Immediately, the cell leader was no longer cooperative. What was his name? Was he a member of Al Qaeda? Where were his weapons? He wasn't talking, but we knew we had our man.

This is where my guys took over. They turned the house upside down, but found nothing. So they started searching the banks of the river—into the tall grass. Even I thought, what the hell are they going to find over there? Lo and behold, on a steep bank along the river they found a hole, covered by a tarp, and covered by tall grass. Jackpot, the weapons and ammo cache. AK-47s, mortar rounds, mortar tubes, remote controls . . . the mother lode. This mortar cell was built not to be found. Safe house in one place. Living quarters in another (that's what we originally raided). Cell leader elsewhere. And weapons underground, along the banks of the river.

The sun was now up. The neighborhood was waking up. We moved quickly. We consolidated our detainees and evidence at the original house and moved out to a hasty PZ. The four birds came back, and we loaded in—Al Qaeda hog-tied and at our feet. The feeling on this ride was different. As the Black Hawks lifted off, my body swelled with relief. All men accounted for. Mission complete.

* * *

On our platoon's first salvo outside the wire, we harvested real bad guys. Wanted, hunted, known bad guys. We discovered and removed a weapons cache. That feeling was greater than any game-winning bucket I had ever shot in my lifetime.

For our mission, the members of my team and I received awards and recognition. That was an honor, but that was not what made that night special to me. What we did together was more important than any recognition could affirm. We adapted. We overcame obstacles. We trusted each other to make decisions that would push the objectives to accomplish our mission. We had our mission success and we put the leader of the terrorist cell and a cache of deadly rockets on ice. We were not individuals: we were a team.

Modern war is defined by ambiguity. The enemy never wears uniforms. The enemy uses women and children as shields—daily. Life-and-death decisions are made at a moment's notice—impacting lives forever. It's messy, almost always.

Ask any combat veteran of Iraq and Afghanistan.

Later in my deployment, I watched Al Qaeda fighters bleed out after a firefight. Should we render aid? Or get real-time intelligence before he breathes his last breath?

We did both. As he was whisked away in the back of a pickup truck, he was an afterthought. Did he live or die? I didn't care then, and I don't care today. He was shooting at us, and our Iraqi allies, so any aid rendered would be grace enough.

My unit experienced devastating scenes back in 2005 and 2006 in Iraq. Confusion and fear surrounded us from all sides. But whenever my guys shot, they did so for a reason. We were in a war, with a mission to fight against a shadowy enemy. Second-guessing was deadly.

I was tasked with releasing Iraqi men who we knew had American blood on their hands. The jagoff lawyers told us we had to do it.

Bet Grandad didn't do that in Normandy.

At the end of my tour—months later!—my last assignment was to fly back to Baghdad and testify against the old man that we rolled up on our first mission outside the wire before I could return home stateside.

That was modern warfare.

That's also how slow the gears of justice worked during the war. The intel we handed over was exploited and good. But lawyers got involved as they did at Gitmo, as they did in Afghanistan, and as they did here. Again, we played by rules—many of them stupid rules, resulting in terrorists walking the streets to kill and kill again.

Did we think about taking justice into our own hands?

Sure we did.

The only thing that truly keeps me up at night is wondering whether those jihadists went on to kill more Americans. Because modern warfighters fight lawyers as much as we fight bad guys. Our enemies should get bullets, not attorneys. The fact that we won't do what is necessary is the reason wars become endless. Modern wars never end, because we won't finish them.

Did my platoon, on that night, have any extremists in our midst? Nope. Just a bunch of Americans—with political viewpoints across the spectrum and skin colors from every share of a Crayon box—united in a shared mission. We were not the extremists; we hunted them. When American troops are given a mission, the men to do it, and the backing of leaders to execute—they will win. That is what modern wars taught me about future wars. That is why I'm with the warfighters—the trigger pullers—every single time. I will have their back, through thick and thin. They will make mistakes, but almost always for the right reason: to bring more of our boys home.

That is our mission. The rest we can't change. That's up to politicians. Our job is to kill the enemy—and when we get rid of the bullshit consuming our military right now, we are the best in the world.

Chapter 11

THE LAWS OF WAR, FOR WINNERS

As I mentioned, I still wake up in the middle of the night with a reoccurring dream. I'm on a mission with my unit, in enemy territory. But I'm racked with anxiety. Where is my weapon? I can't find my rifle. I'm hoping nobody will notice, as I do everything I can do to find my weapon. It's lost. I'm helpless.

It's an irrational dream, but I can't shake it. I've never lost my weapon in combat, or training. But I know what the consequence would be. Not only would I be combat ineffective and receive universal scorn, but it would also be career ending (or career-altering, at best). If a junior leader, or any combat troop, loses their weapon—they throw the book at you. Loss of position, loss of rank, loss of pay. The Army will hold you accountable, that much a soldier can count on. Other services, with other "sensitive items," do the same thing.

My unit in Iraq once cleared an entire city to try to find a 240B machine gun that had been lost in a complex IED ambush conducted on our

Scout Platoon. It was a foolish and counterproductive exercise, but we did it anyway. Our battalion commander wanted his weapon back, mostly because it was his hide if it was lost—even in combat.

But what if a general—or lots of generals—lost billions of dollars of military equipment? Specifically, $7 billion worth of equipment? 10,000 air-to-ground munitions . . . 40,000 military vehicles, including 12,000 Humvees . . . 300,000 personal weapons . . . unknown number of communications equipment . . . 42,000 pieces of night vision, surveillance, and biometric and positioning equipment . . . 17,500 pieces of explosive detection equipment . . . and at least 73 aircraft. All lost. And not just lost, but in the hands of our avowed enemy. The same enemy who killed two thousand Americans over twenty years—the last thirteen to a suicide bombing that was completely preventable.

That's what happened in Afghanistan in 2021. Lives lost. Weapons lost. Allies abandoned. And America humiliated, in utter defeat and retreat.

Not one general was fired for this. Not even demoted or reprimanded. The only person who was fired was a Marine Corps lieutenant colonel— Stuart Scheller—who had the courage to speak out about the lack of accountability. He was promptly . . . fired.

Rules for thee, but not for me. The troops have always, for good reason, distrusted the "brass" but they've never had more reason than today. The gulf between private to general has never been wider. Generals in World War II were fired. Generals in Vietnam were fired. But not generals today. No matter how poor their performance, they get that promotion—and especially that sweetheart defense contractor job after retirement. "Joe" (not Biden, the rank and file) deals with half-baked social theories implemented at the unit level, knowing somewhere a general is getting promoted for doing the foolish bidding of an ignorant and/or ideological politician.

An ineffective, woke, unaccountable military is an affront—at every level—to the young men who actually pull the triggers. Their job gets more difficult, less satisfying, and a lot more chaotic. And then people die. Joe knows where to point the finger—and it's a middle finger.

What's most galling is that these same leaders who betrayed our objectives in Afghanistan—and the honor of our country—love to lecture every Western nation that violates hopelessly outdated international laws.

Part of the problem is that they conflate international law with just war theory. They think they are one and the same, and make us all dumber in the process. So what is a just war theory?

Simply, a doctrine that theorizes the ethics of the combatant. Some trace it as far back as ancient Egypt. Saint Augustine wrote in the classic *City of God*, over four hundred years after Christ's death:

> *They who have waged war in obedience to the divine command,*
> *or in conformity with His laws, have represented in their persons*
> *the public justice or the wisdom of government, and in this capac-*
> *ity have put to death wicked men; such persons have by no means*
> *violated the commandment, "Thou shalt not kill."*

Saint Augustine, coincidentally during the time when Christians were being persecuted, articulated a way that God called his followers to be proactive toward evil. He believed that war was not inherently evil but, if done in the name of righteousness and for the proper reasons, was something God required us to do.

To quote Dietrich Bonhoeffer, who was later executed by the Third Reich for living up to his words, "Silence in the face of evil is itself evil. God will not hold us guiltless. Not to speak is to speak. Not to act is to act."

Jus ad bellum, established in the UN Charter after World War II, lays out the conditions under which states may resort to war. It's how you go to war justly. Once the firing starts, modern countries are directed to follow the "laws of war," referred to as *Jus in bello.* This is how you fight war justly. It was supposed to be a global remedy—a rulebook—to end senseless violence.

Before you break glass for war, *Jus ad bellum* asks:

Is this a just cause? Do you have the right authority? Do you maintain the right intention? Is there a reason for the chance of success? Will you display proportionality? Is this a last resort?

Then, once you are separating meat from bone in battle, once the carnage has commenced, *jus in bello* asks: Are you fighting with proportionality? Are you discriminating between civilian and military targets? Are the objectives strictly military?

World War I was so brutal, so unabashed, there was a clamoring for some formally imposed restrictions on what countries could do to each other. The Geneva Conventions became a *Jus in bello* international law of sorts. Limiting the barbarity of conflict between nations. Guaranteeing that a military force would wear a uniform. Honor a chain of command. The conventions post–World War I established what would happen if you surrendered on the battlefield. The conventions signed at Geneva were to make humane what was never thought of to be humane: warfare.

With "rules" in war, if you wear a uniform and surrender, all your soldiers will also put down their rifles.

More lives are spared.

If you wear a uniform, you don't fire on civilians who are not in uniform.

More lives are spared.

And if you promise to protect soldiers who surrender, more soldiers will be incentivized to not fight to the death.

More lives are spared.

The problem with "international law," of course, is that there's no such thing as international police to enforce it. The key question of our generation—of the wars in Iraq and Afghanistan—is way more complicated: What do you do if your enemy does not honor the Geneva Conventions? We asked it all the time—especially if we want to win. And, for all the briefings, PowerPoint slide decks, and lectures, it was never clear.

We never got an answer. Only more war. More casualties. And no victory.

Should we follow the Geneva Conventions? What if we treated the enemy the way they treated us? Would that not be an incentive for the other side to reconsider their barbarism? Hey, Al Qaeda: If you surrender, we *might* spare your life. If you do not, we will rip your arms off and feed them to hogs.

Makes me wonder, in 2024—if you want to win—how can anyone write universal rules about killing other people in open conflict? Especially against enemies who fight like savages, disregarding human life in every single instance. Maybe, instead, we are just fighting with one hand behind our back—and the enemy knows it.

This is a big reason there hasn't been a war declared globally since the 1950s and, quite frankly, why America hasn't won a war since World War II.

If the world cannot agree on principles of honor or morality, how can we ever prescribe global terms of fair war? Land warfare, historically understood, is defined by how many people you can slaughter in one space, at one time—limiting the *will and capacity* of your enemy to fight. (Same goes for bombing, missiles, and drone strikes; just a different delivery mechanism.) War will never be anything but hell as long as human nature stays deceptive, vengeful, and angry. Much to the chagrin of utopians and progressives, human nature has not changed. And will not change. We are flawed. We are sinful. Men will *always* fight other men.

Many efforts to curb the blood lust on the battlefield have been attempted. The Kellogg-Briand Pact of 1928, which was essentially betrayed hours after the ink dried on it, tried to assure that nations would not use war to resolve conflicts. It did nothing to prevent World War II yet was used to sentence Japanese and German soldiers and officers to death in the aftermath of the conflict that it had so egregiously failed to prevent. Article 51 of the United Nations made war legal only if you were attacked. The escalation of that war was left TBD—to be determined. Illegal wars continued, and violence still escalated.

If our warriors are forced to follow rules arbitrarily and asked to sacrifice more lives so that international tribunals feel better about themselves, *aren't we just better off winning our wars according to our own rules?!* Who cares what other countries think. The question we have to ask ourselves is, if we are forced to fight, are we going to fight to win? Or will we fight to make leftists feel good—which means not wining and fighting forever.

In this context, the Europeans are the worst. Outdated, outgunned, invaded, and impotent. Why should America, the European "emergency contact number" for the past century, listen to self-righteous and impotent nations asking us to honor outdated and one-sided defense arrangements they no longer live up to? Maybe if NATO countries actually ponied up for their own defense—but they don't. They just yell about the rules while gutting their militaries and yelling at America for help.

History regards the Greatest Generation not for their poetry, artistic endeavors, or their culinary brilliance. That title was bestowed because they were two-time world war champions. They were great because they understood they were at war and that the consequence for losing the war was annihilation. They killed the enemy. Sometimes in ways that would offend modern sensibilities. Two nuclear bombs ended a war that could have dragged on for years, costing millions more *American* lives. They won. Who cares.

We have watered down the last twenty years of armed conflict into morality plays over what "should have happened" and how a "morally superior" person should react when their friends become pink mist from an Iranian-built, Chinese-financed roadside bomb. We send men to fight on our behalf, and then second-guess the manner in which they fight. I saw it every day. In some cases our units were so boxed in by rules and regulations and political correctness, we even second-guess ourselves. That needs to end. Count me out on the Monday morning quarterbacking— I'm with the American warfighter, all the way.

As of the writing of this book, the Biden administration made the lives of warfighters even more difficult. In opposition to long-standing DoD policy—and bending to international pressure—the Biden administration changed the policy on civilians on the battlefield. For decades, the United States opposed any international-law presumption that "persons or objects in combat zones are civilians." Especially in modern times, the battlefield is complex—and the enemy uses that against us. They never want to fight us toe to toe; civilians are central to their strategy.

Making such a presumption endangers American troops and gives an advantage to savage enemies—who don't play by the rules. *Citing no new evidence*, the Biden administration simply reversed course in July 2023. Now persons and objects in combat zones—in places where US troops are fighting—must be presumed to be *civilian*. They must be assumed to be *innocent*. In short, this means our troops are going to have to hesitate every time they fire. This change reminds me of the stupid legal brief we received at FOB Falcon in Baghdad in 2005. Bad ideas have been around for a long time, but now they're fully institutionalized.

When you send Americans to war, their mandate *should be* to lethally dominate the battlefield. If that makes you uneasy, keep us at home.

I could write five thousand more words on the ins and outs of the philosophy of warfare, the folly of international law, and the crazy maze of rules of engagement. I've heard it all. And I've seen a lot of it. I've guarded Islamists. I was a platoon leader in combat. I worked with local forces. Met with indigenous political leaders. I taught counterinsurgency in Afghanistan when the strategy was clearly not working. I was pro-surge, in both Iraq and Afghanistan. I've stood over dead enemy and stood in front of battlefield crosses. War is hell, and full of shades of gray. And, no doubt, personal morality weighs heavily on each individual soul.

But if we're going to send our boys to fight—and it should be boys—we need to unleash them to win. They need them to be the most ruthless. The most uncompromising. The most overwhelmingly lethal as they can be. We must break the enemy's will. Our troops will make mistakes, and when they do, they should get the overwhelming benefit of the doubt.

Hence why this book talks so much about leadership—especially generals. If our generals are focused on woke priorities, they are not focused on warfighting. Which means, when the bullets start flying, they will throw our troops right under the international bus. The next commander in chief will need to clean house—and rewrite these laws (much as President Trump did when he unleashed the military to defeat ISIS).

And one more thing . . . the next president should also change the name of the Department of Defense back to the War Department. Sure, our military defends us. And in a perfect world it exists to deter threats and preserve peace. But ultimately its job is to conduct war. We either win or lose wars. And we have warriors, not "defenders." Bringing back the War Department may remind a few people in Washington, DC, what the military is supposed to do, and do well.

Our boys should not fight by rules written by dignified men in mahogany rooms eighty years ago. America should fight by its own rules. And we should fight to win, or not go at all.

Chapter 12

HARVARD AND GENERALS: A LOVE STORY

One of the greatest American soldiers to ever live was Joshua Chamberlain, of the 20th Maine Infantry Regiment. During the battle of Little Round Top, a part of the larger Battle of Gettysburg in the Civil War, he led his men in a furious firefight to defend the Union flank from wave after wave of rebels. Finally, seeing his men were nearly out of ammunition, Chamberlain ordered a bayonet charge, which sent the Confederates running. During the fighting, he noticed another soldier—a deserter whose life he had spared. Chamberlain had assigned the man to be flag bearer for the unit, a post of honor. This show of respect for an ordinary man under his command had paid off.

Chamberlain later recalled seeing Sergeant Andrew Tozier's courage in a citation recommending him for the Medal of Honor:

When our whole center was for a moment broken and the enemy seemed about to overpower us, I saw, as a thick cloud of smoke lifted, Sergeant Tozier standing alone . . . the color staff rested on the ground and supported in the hollow of his shoulder, while with a musket and cartridge box he had picked up at his feet, he was defending his color, presenting a figure which seemed to have paralyzed the enemy in front of him, who might otherwise have captured the color.

Before the war, Chamberlain was a college professor who had taught rhetoric at Bowdoin College. But he'd always wanted to be a soldier. In that eloquent citation, Chamberlain's skill with language—his expertise, and his reputation as a warrior—melded into one great heroic effort to support a strong man.

Such an attitude is totally foreign to the landscape of America's modern elite.

* * *

Every major invasion requires a foothold. The beaches of Normandy, in the summer of 1944, saw thousands of boots pour into German defenses. Weeks later the bloodied beaches of Normandy had been transformed into a major American depot for supplies, reinforcements, and armored vehicles. Yesterday's battlefield can easily become tomorrow's base of operations.

In 2010—under Barack Obama—the Left needed another foothold in their goal to transform the fabric of our nation, and the military was low-hanging fruit. As such, women in combat and the repeal of "Don't Ask, Don't Tell" became the drumbeat for their systematic change.

That same year, on July 1, I was asked to testify at the Supreme Court confirmation hearing for Elena Kagan—President Obama's second appointment to the high court. I was a veteran, who was currently attending graduate school—two facts that were pertinent to *her* background. The Republicans asked me to testify, and I agreed. Before I knew it, Senate Judiciary Committee chairman Patrick Leahy (D-Vermont) was saying my name and asking if he pronounced it correctly.

"Yes, sir," was my response, but I didn't press the microphone to pick it up. Instead, I took a swig from my bottled water, took a breath, and settled in as a witness for a confirmation hearing for an associate justice with a lifetime appointment for America's highest court.

During Justice Kagan's confirmation hearing I was a graduate student at Harvard University. The same Harvard that then Dean Kagan used as a cudgel to attack the military when she decided to bar all military recruiters from campus due to her objection to the Clinton-era "Don't Ask, Don't Tell" policy on homosexuals in the military. She also completely flaunted a federal law guaranteeing recruiters equal access to schools. As CNN's Bill Mears wrote during the confirmation hearings,

> *Just four months after taking the job as Harvard's dean, in October 2003, Kagan offered students her thoughts in a campuswide e-mail, saying that to give recruiters equal access to the campus "causes me deep distress. I abhor the military's discriminatory recruitment policy." She called it "a profound wrong—a moral injustice of the first order."*

At the witness table, I was speaking as a citizen and a Soldier. As I often do when I speak publicly, I reflected on my men and our mission. In the beginning of my opening remarks, I laid out the central question: "In replacing the only remaining veteran on the Supreme Court [Justice John Paul Stevens], how did we reach this point in this country where we're nominating someone who unapologetically obstructed the military at a time of war? Ms. Kagan chose to use her position of authority to impede, rather than to empower, the warriors who have fought, and who have fallen, for this country." That was why this mattered. But a more particular policy point is what was most hotly contested.

Also at issue in this hearing were concurrent attempts to repeal "Don't Ask, Don't Tell" that I, and others, believed were an attempt to pry open the culture of the U.S. military and make our fighting formations look more like our failing universities. "Don't Ask, Don't Tell" was an imperfect formulation, everyone agreed. It was a compromise—to keep military distractions to a minimum, yet allow all Americans to wear the uniform. Our warriors had these rules not to prove some ideological point, but because more important things were at stake.

Furthermore, the rules that Kagan so vigorously contended against were rules governed by the civilian leadership of the nation, specifically President Bill Clinton, whom Kagan worked for from 1995 to 1999, first as associate White House counsel and then as deputy assistant to the president for domestic policy and deputy director of the Domestic Policy Council (DPC).

Did Kagan have a problem with the policy or with the military? And why would she attack recruitment? Did she really believe that a military recruiter could outfox a Harvard student and manipulate them into serving their country against their own interests? As Senator Jeff Sessions stated during the hearings,

"Don't Ask, Don't Tell" was created and implemented by President Clinton. Where was her outrage during the five years she served in the Clinton White House? Why would she blame the military? They didn't pass the rule. It was Congress and the president. . . . Instead of taking a stand in Washington, Ms. Kagan waited until

she got to Harvard and stood in the way of devoted, hardworking military recruiters.

Our professional all-volunteer force exists for a reason. With two foreign wars raging after 9/11, our military needed access to recruiting the "best and brightest" our nation has to offer. Put yourself in Elena Kagan's shoes. Why would you not want the military to offer your students an opportunity to serve their nation at war? (Well, it was Harvard, after all. Most of those kids were too fat, and too dumb, to serve anyway. High on confidence, low on common sense. Trust me, I've been there. But I digress.)

For most of America's history, the military was comprised of volunteer recruits only. In 1812, with the threat of another war brewing, President James Monroe wanted to draft Americans to prepare us for the pending war against Great Britain. The House and Senate accused him of being a Napoleonic tyrant for considering that solution even while facing an existential crisis that would result in the devastation of Washington, DC, and the torching of the White House. Conscription was considered a violation of freedom in the early days of our Republic.

Americans stayed away from conscription until 1840, when the Selective Training and Service (STS) Act required all men ages twenty-one to forty-five to register for the draft. At that time nearly half (47 percent) of our fighting forces were composed of Irish and German immigrants. While the STS Act required all men to register, the draft was not implemented until the Civil War.

During the American Civil War, approximately 250,000 Union soldiers were drafted. Of that number approximately 87,000 of those drafted paid a fee to get out of service, while 117,000 affluent Americans hired someone to go in their place. Of the Union soldiers drafted, only 46,000 actually served in combat against the Confederate States.

Volunteers have always won America's wars. Which is a big problem today, because it is increasingly clear the Left doesn't want Americans—or at least certain Americans—to volunteer for the military.

The definition of duty and public service has changed radically. Today, more Americans would volunteer for an experimental vaccine than would join the military. We have seen how the radical Left wants to change the fabric of the nation, now they are aiming toward another pillar of America: her defense. And what is most alarming is that the Left is receiving aid and comfort from the civilian leadership and field grade officers who are constitutionally required to protect the very institution they seem hell-bent on destroying. If quietly, and with different explosives, our Joint Chiefs are doing to our military what Al Qaeda did to the Golden Dome Mosque in 2006 in Samarra, Iraq. I witnessed both, and both are sabotage.

This attack on our military ethos, on our warriors, from these cultural arsonists is not just an assault on our institutions. It also isn't just a political statement that America isn't worth the effort. This is a statement on the blood that has already been spilt in previous wars. This assault is just another unprovoked, but intentional, move to cheapen our fallen heroes' legacy—and then neuter our future.

This was all on my mind as I shuffled papers to stand against the nomination of Justice Elena Kagan for the Supreme Court. To cover her tracks, Justice Kagan said all the right patriotic platitudes a politician would say about a military at war. We are used to such pandering. But when it counted, when she had the opportunity to back those words up with actions as dean of Harvard, she didn't just turn her back, she went out of her way to keep the Harvard students far away from an opportunity to serve.

The 2005 opposition to military lawyers visiting Harvard Law school, which was championed by Kagan, occurred during the toughest fighting in Iraq and Afghanistan. It also happened while the nation was dealing with legal issues (mostly led by weak-kneed, America-hating ACLU types) concerning enemy combatants, "international rights" of illegal combatants, and the beginnings of extrajudicial drone attacks. Not to mention the debate about the "rights" of assholes (I mean, "detainees") at Gitmo. A place I knew well.

Other legal issues had arisen concerning the newly approved Patriot Act and the use of personal data gleaned from Americans overseas and at home. Why wouldn't Harvard want its students to be a part of these solutions? Why wouldn't they want their opinions and interests to be reflected in real-time decision making? (Now, of course, I want no leftist Harvard lawyers anywhere near the military—but the principle still stands.)

Bottom line: while America was at war, Kagan was busy fighting against the JAG Corps and using Harvard students as useful idiots in the battle.

Some tried to argue that because JAG officers were eventually allowed on campus, it showed there wasn't a problem; those people ignore that this never should have been a debate. JAG had always been allowed on campus, until Dean Kagan blocked them. It was only after her dictate was overruled by the university, and Kagan buckled at the threat from the DoD to take back the almost half of billion dollars of federal taxpayer funding Harvard University received that year, that JAG was allowed to return. Kagan responded to the money, but she still supported, encouraged, and welcomed the radical student protest that kept JAG officers from recruiting at her school.

For years Harvard stayed out of these matters, but under Dean Elena Kagan, the university joined a friend-of-the-court brief opposing the 1994 Solomon Amendment, which was what allowed the DoD to threaten to withhold federal funds over access to recruitment. Under

Kagan, Harvard also bused students to DC to assist in protesting and lobbying efforts to overturn "Don't Ask, Don't Tell."

There I sat at the confirmation hearing. So I pointed out the red herring argument:

> *As a legal scholar, she knows better than that. She knows that the policy she abhors is not the military's policy, but a policy enacted by Congress and imposed on the military. In fact, after the law was passed, Ms. Kagan went to work for the very man who signed "Don't Ask, Don't Tell" into law—President Clinton. So for her to call it "the military's policy" is intellectually dishonest, and her opposition to military recruiters at Harvard Law School had the effect of shooting the messenger.*
>
> *Likewise, while Ms. Kagan sought to block full access to military recruiters, she welcomed to campus numerous Senators and Congressmen who voted for the law she calls "a moral injustice of the first order." Additionally, Harvard Law School has three academic chairs endowed by money from Saudi Arabia, a country where being a homosexual is a capital offense. So, rather than confront the Congressional source of the policy—or take a stand against a country that executes homosexuals—Ms. Kagan zeroed in on military recruiters for a policy they neither authored, nor emphasized.*

This wasn't about policy for Ms. Kagan. This was about the military itself. As the old saying goes, "scratch a liberal, get an America-hating socialist peacenik." Okay, maybe it's not an old saying, but it fits Kagan. She doesn't like the military, especially if it won't bend to her will. To Kagan, the military is *below* Harvard. Harvard kids work for hedge funds and NGOs, not heavy-artillery units or with NVGs (night-vision goggles).

* * *

Under the guise of a policy dispute, but really in pursuit of something else, "Don't Ask, Don't Tell" was just the beginning. Of course, the Left moved the goalposts even further once DADT was repealed. It's what they always do—and, no matter what, the military will never be woke enough for them to support it.

DADT was a controversial policy. And we all know the Obama administration overturned it. At the time, I was mostly ambivalent. It just wasn't a big issue for me. I didn't really have a problem with DADT, and I didn't have a big problem with overturning DADT. In fact, I was mobilizing for deployment to Afghanistan at Fort Dix, New Jersey, when the new policy was being unveiled across "big Army." Our commander briefed the unit, peppered with a few jokes. You know, infantry stuff. We mostly laughed it off and moved on. America was at war. Gays and lesbians were already serving in the military. I had seen the enemy with my own eyes. We needed everybody.

I now regret that passive perspective.

Not because I have a newfound ax to grind with gay Americans. But because I naïvely believed that's what ending "Don't Ask, Don't Tell" was all about. Once again, our good faith was used against us. The Left never gives an inch, and always takes a mile.

The establishment of DADT, and then ending of DADT, were just policy footholds for radical Leftists, hell-bent on even more radical social change—a full-frontal attack on almost every institution of the military. The initial policy was imposed by politicians, but as the Left grew more extreme, they needed it to be the military's fault. Once the Left was successful in rewriting history to claim the military enacted DADT in the first place, instead of the political class in Washington, then the same revisionists used that momentum to push for the next military mea culpa: the reversal of DADT altogether.

This is not just my opinion, as a conservative, straight infantryman. While writing this book, I interviewed an Army veteran who was on the political front line of fighting to end DADT. As a closeted enlisted soldier, this individual joined other gay and lesbian soldiers to protest in front of the White House for the end of DADT. His words are instructive:

> *At that moment, from where I was coming from—if we have qualified gays and lesbians in the military—of course they should be able to serve and be out of the closet. We didn't get much push back. But here's the thing, that push seemed to be the tipping point for all this other shit to start. This is when all the radical trans stuff started. Even during the DADT repeal, they were trying to slip in the trans stuff—but it didn't get into the military until now. We didn't want that stuff, but ideologues did.*
>
> *What started under Obama, I think, was when the military became collateral damage. Everything went crazy, and as a result it made its way throughout the military. A lot of what we're seeing in the Biden era, is a reaction to the evil of Trump. Now the genie is out of the bottle, it went so crazy. I was inadvertently used to issue in a bunch of crap that I wasn't in for. A lot of the DADT repeal movement people are no longer in the public eye. Gay guys who wanted to serve openly, but that didn't mean they were pushing for the nonsense. So, yes, you feel used. Used to usher in the gender cult.*

He concluded, "The 'trans and gender cults stuff'" hurts readiness, it doesn't help it. "We have too many partisan hacks running policy in our military that have no connection to fighting or soldiering."

He's right, and my interviews with dozens of other veterans confirm the same. The repeal of DADT was the breach in the wire—the foothold—the Left needed to push *much more* extreme ideology through the gap. During the Obama administration, I personally heard from sitting senators and members of Congress that transgenders would *never* stand in front of formations wearing the uniform of their chosen gender. That was fantasy. A false flag, I was told. And regarding women in combat, I was assured: "We are not barbarians. Women can serve, and are important. But no one wants to see women in the infantry," one *liberal* member of Congress told me. Fools, all of them.

Secretary of Defense Robert Gates, who served under both Presidents Bush and Obama, in his book *Duty* details his recollection of the time in 2011 when President Obama wanted to repeal the DADT military policy. Secretary Gates was worried about the impact of the repeal of DADT on readiness, recruiting, and retention. He knew how important it was to continue the kinetic tempo of Iraq and Afghanistan and did not want our fighting force unnecessarily distracted by the imposition of a partisan political policy intended to win support in blue states instead of winning a war in the Middle East. President Obama simply did not care. This was a political scalp the president needed to take. The military was just a background for policies. And we wonder why ISIS took Toyotas across Iraq without resistance and how Kabul fell faster than a northern California redwood?

* * *

Learning is a good thing. But intellectualism and intelligence aren't synonyms. You have to be willing to get your hands dirty to translate learning into wisdom. Alexander the Great learned from Aristotle as a boy, but he also led from the front. At the same time, Genghis Khan, the rare uneducated military genius, was able to conquer vast amounts of the known world while not a single general working for him had a master's degree or PhD. He also didn't have to carry his vaccination card to deploy.

We need Alexander the Greats studying with Aristotles. Or, at least, that used to be true. I used to think it was a good thing that—for decades—almost every senior military officer was encouraged to attend graduate school at an "elite" university. Mostly, because civilians might learn something about the military. But the opposite happened—our military leaders didn't learn real knowledge from civilians; they learned how to think like civilians. And too many of them contracted the woke mind virus. The majors and colonels who go to left-wing colleges later become the generals and commanders who diligently push the lunacy of higher education, with top-cover from their political leaders. They still wear camouflage; it just has a pink hue to it. This is being done know-ingly. Purposely. The military had to look more like Harvard, and less like Heartbreak Ridge. And it has worked.

The Obama administration easily manipulated the feckless and po-liticized military brass that offered little resistance to his radical policies. Once in the Beltway, armed with their newfound academic appreciation for politically correct notions, lifelong officers became willing executers for politicians. In fact, it was the quickest way to get promoted. Their value was not in their devotion to the Constitution or the warrior class, but in their willingness to take orders from a superstar president. They loved being declared "bold" and "fresh" by the media more than they desired to execute their duties to the Army. They went to graduate school with that same media, after all.

After the repeal of "Don't Ask, Don't Tell," the next policy the Left pushed was women in combat. While the American people had always rejected the radical-feminist so-called "Equal Rights Amendment," Team Obama could fast-track their social engineering through the military's top-down chain of command. The military could implement its designs and outcomes without oversight. What military leader would stand in the way of empowerment and sexual revolution? Certainly not Harvard-educated two-star generals?

What is it about this time in American history that has given us so many feckless generals? Why would leaders who have served honorably for over thirty years now decide to completely abandon all their commitments and previously proclaimed values to be on the right side of a political narrative? Or the "right side of history"? American history abounds with generals who decided that their honor and fidelity were more important than surviving a political storm. They stepped away from their posts rather than retreating from their convictions. The answer is pretty straightforward: courage has surrendered to safety, merit surrendered to equity, and honor surrendered to ideology. Careers, not the Constitution, are the highest calling of our general class. To save themselves, they have surrendered our warriors.

Over fifteen years ago, it became fashionable to attack the Iraq War. As a veteran fresh home from combat, I ran a veterans group that wanted to win the wars. Maybe naïve, but it was honest—and focused *only* on the warriors, their war, and our country. Little did I know at the time, but I wasn't just debating the status of the war: I was debating the purpose of why our military exists. Senators, generals, and pundits would eagerly accept an invitation to debate an infantry junior officer fresh home from the Iraqi dust. One such occasion was a debate I attended in London—the Spectator/Intelligence Squared debate—on the future of Iraq in 2007. In front of a BBC worldwide audience of over one billion viewers, Tony Benn, William Shawcross, Sir Christopher Meyer, Ali Allawi, Rory Stewart, and a very young, 1LT Peter Hegseth debated the future of Iraq.

I made the mistake—time and time again—of thinking that we

were really debating the merits of the war in good faith. What I missed, and that gets clearer every single day, is that the radical left wing of America was—and will always be—in a permanent state of war, but only with their domestic opponents, not their foreign enemies. They believe the purpose of the military is to enact domestic policy and chalk up wins over their culture war opponents, not defend the nation and the Constitution. I would mic up for a spirited interview with retired generals and left-wing veterans on Chris Matthews's *Hardball* and listen as a debate about Iraq policy would tumble into non sequitur dissertations about feminism, green energy solutions, and socialized medicine.

One would think that if you wanted free health care, free education, hell, even citizenship, the military wouldn't be the group you would want to attack. In a reasonable world, a capable military—especially at a time of war—would be an area for agreement. Instead, it worked the other way around. The original sin of the military was that they expect soldiers to actually earn their benefits, and the Left could never tolerate a meritocracy built on serving a power greater than partisan leadership.

* * *

This wasn't just about the war—this was about the warrior. There was plenty of disagreement to be had about the Iraq War, and I've admitted on many occasions that I missed the forest for the trees on many of my Iraq War assessments. But while I debated these things in good faith, the Left mobilized. Electing Obama, railroading the military, pushing women in combat—readiness be damned. The Left has never fought fair.

Ordinary American patriots are left hanging out to dry. It's a tale as old as time. Do you know what happened to Sergeant Andrew Tozier after the Civil War ended? Illiterate and living on a meager pension, he became a criminal, channeling his warrior skills to a bad purpose by robbing clothing stores and rustling cattle. Eventually caught, he was sentenced to five years in prison, only to be unexpectedly pardoned by the governor of Maine . . . none other than Joshua Chamberlain. Chamberlain did more than that: he took Tozier and his wife in to live with his own family for years, employed them, worked to reform Tozier, and taught him to read. Afterward, Tozier became a farmer and the subject of the Maine state song.

As I finished my opening statement on July 1, 2010, at the confirmation hearing for Elena Kagan, I thought back to how the powerful use the impressionable to push their agenda. How could I express my patriotism and my passionate disagreement with a side that believes that I am the enemy?

Sure, the Iraq War wasn't perfect—and in retrospect it didn't unleash much good. Many experts in military history and academia will tell you that the biggest mistake after 9/11 was opening a second front in Iraq. They are probably right.

But, as we look back on twenty years of war, perhaps the biggest mistake wasn't opening a second front in the Middle East. It was ignoring the third front that the Left opened at home while 1 percent of my generation was fighting street by street, block by block.

I don't blame the Left. Like Elena Kagan, we know who they are now. They always wanted to make our military woke and weak. Their sins I now understand. The biggest sin, and most unforgiveable, was that we—the military—allowed it to occur.

Chapter 13

THE BROKEN AMERICAN COVENANT

Our Founders were not universally orthodox Christians as much as they were aficionados of covenantal communities. They believed that great peoples had organizing principles that were larger than their tribal connections or their family ties. While most of them had deep Christian beliefs, they were also predominantly English settlers, who had experienced the hardships and traumas of denominational sectarianism.

The history of England was plagued with politicized versions of denominational sovereignty that executed godly Christian men at the hands of monarchial privilege. The English-bred Americans might have been Protestant Christians, but they did not seek to gather people around specific religious agreement. Their ancestors had played that game and had extracted buckets of blood in the attempt to gather around a common faith.

The American Founders did not ascribe to a tribal fidelity, nor a fidelity based on a monarch or a holy family, nor on a particular religious denomination. Instead, our unique system of government was modeled after the covenantal approach of the Old Testament nation of Israel, which was fulfilled in the New Testament covenant of Christ. A government based not on blood, but on a structured, written law, freely ascribed to and affirmed by each person as a condition of citizenry and fidelity. The Constitution of United States of America was conceived as our secular covenant, our Law. The Founders placed an enormous amount of weight on the fact that it was not possible to take a public leadership role, or take on a function of government, without publicly swearing an oath to the document that binds us together in law and covenant.

In the Bible, the Covenant of Israel was an agreement between God and Israel that if Israel kept the commands of God (most often recognized as the 613 commands of the Torah), then God would preserve the peace of the people in the Promised Land. It was a conditional covenant with both blessings and curses connected with the behaviors of the people.

The book of Deuteronomy frames the Covenant with Israel with a national meeting of the Jewish people at Shechem in chapters 27 and beyond. Within those chapters, and in many of the other biblical covenants, the people of God affirm that their blessings are reliant upon their adherence to the Laws that God has given to them. If they reject the Laws of God, then they will lose their blessings and receive curses commensurate to the violations incurred.

This is the moral universe of the Old Testament. The people have been given the Law from God. The reception of the Law is what makes them exceptional. They are a people who have been called out of Babylon with Abraham and called out of Egypt with Moses.

What makes them distinct is not so much their birth but their commitment to the principles set out in the Covenant that God has given to them. They are to keep the Law so they may be kept in the favor of God and in the comfort of the blessings that cascade from the Covenant itself. If they keep the Law, then their futures are protected by God; if they reject the Law and return to the ways of their forefathers in the pagan world, they will not only lose their blessings, but they will also be cursed by God—for generations.

One biblical story illustrates the story of a people struggling to maintain their covenant with God. The story of Gideon took place in a nation that was unprotected by a strong and trained military, with those who rose to defend themselves wielding simple field tools to ward off armed invaders from neighboring villages.

The problem was that Gideon was a farmer who was called to lead an army of farmers and shepherds against a professional army, and you can see his hesitance in his repeated attempts to get out of fulfilling God's calling. It only got worse from there. Instead of finding comfort in the training and equipping of a 32,000-man army, Gideon found himself following God's order to pare down the number of his forces so that Israel would not boast that "our own strength has delivered us" (Judges 7:2). So God instructed Gideon to tell the men that whoever was afraid should go home. This instruction alone eliminated 22,000 men from Gideon's army.

Now with only 10,000 brave men, Gideon's army would be ready to fight the Midianites. But God's army had even more cuts to make before the final battle.

The Lord spoke to Gideon again, "There are still too many men. Bring them down to the water and I will thin the ranks some more. When I say, 'This one should not go with you, do not take him.'"

God instructed Gideon to send the men to the water to drink. Those who drank the water by bringing a cupped hand to their mouths remained in the army, while those who dropped to their knees, bowed their head and their eyes, and lapped up the water to drink were sent home. Scholars debate the reason: Was cupping the water more civilized? Did it mean their eyes remained up, able to scan for the enemy while drinking? Or was God simply eliminating a large group of thirsty men from the ranks of the army? Either way, the army was full of men who lapped up the water. The final elimination of men left Gideon's army with only three hundred men to face the Midianite army.

One would think that the elimination of 31,700 men from their combat forces would be enough to show the Israelite people that God was their only strength and shield before the Midianite army, but God was not done hamstringing the army of Gideon.

Gideon was instructed to break his forces into three units of one hundred men. They would be sent into the camp of the Midianites during the darkest hour of the evening. But instead of sending the army into the camp with sword and shield in hand, Gideon instructs his men to approach the camp with a torch in a clay jar in one hand and a trumpet in the other. Like Joshua at the battle of Jericho, Gideon was instructed to use sound and visual drama to take down the enemy.

When the trumpets sounded and the torches came to life, the Midianite camp was sent into a panic. They assumed that the torches and trumpets represented only a portion of the attacking army, and with no visual evidence to the contrary, the Midianites began to scatter and attack each other.

God and the army of Gideon had sown panic and disruption into the Midianite army and God used that panic to rout the army without the need for the invading Israelites to draw their own weapons. In the days that followed, Gideon put out a call to his kinsmen to track down and eliminate the scattered and frightened army as they approached the boundaries of the water and tribal regions of Israel. The faithful Army of God would vanquish the enemy.

Gideon emerges as a warrior who trusts in the Lord completely and who leads an army armed only with lamps and trumpets to defeat their enemies by the power of God's direction and divine persuasion. It was a story of a military expedition in which the people were called by God, narrowed by God, and then sent to win a battle that only God could win. Ultimately, it was meant to draw Israel closer into the arms of God.

* * *

It is only the survivors of war who can ask their family members, like in the famous finale of *Saving Private Ryan*, "Tell me I am good man." When a covenantal warrior—an American soldier—is preparing for combat, we are confident, righteous, and good. We believe we are on the right side of battle and enter combat with a clear conscience.

Moreover, we enter military life to show ourselves worthy—to be seen as valorous. To meet the challenge of our time and to defend our fellow citizens who are innocent and weak. To protect the homeland, our families, and our way of life. When we maintain our covenant, we are Gideon—God on our side, heroism and victory in our future.

But what if we ignore our covenant? We turn our backs . . . on each other.

America today is in a cold civil war. Our soul is under attack by a confederacy of radicals. They wish to erode our institutions by making us question our purpose. They seek to make us believe that everything we have is somehow taken from other people's efforts, other people's possessions. *Stolen land! Patriarchy! Racism!* That we are tribal by nature, and hopelessly divided. That America is not that great; was never great. And, for the purposes of this book, that the US military is a tool for conquest, imperialism, and oppression.

The unique nature of Gideon's story was not revealed to me until many years after I came home from war overseas. In fact, I was only reminded of it during a sermon my family attended at a small church in the panhandle of Florida a few years ago. Like many of us, I had heard the children's Sunday school version. And it seemed like it should be enough, but it's not enough. "There is," as the famous radio voice Paul Harvey used to say, ". . . the rest of the story."

And the rest of the story is devastating.

The rest of the story tells us that God didn't just demand that Gideon would contend against the Midianite enemy, but well before Gideon fought the foreign enemy he would have to contend with the enemy at home. Gideon's own tribe, his own village, his own family were worshipping the Midianite gods. They had set up altars to Baal, and an Asherah pole in the center of the village square. Gideon's initial call from God was to be courageous enough to stand up for the Law of God and show the people that there should be no false gods before Jehovah.

So before he leads his men under cover of night into the camp of the Midianites, he enters the village square under cover of night, then he and ten other men cut down the Asherah pole, destroy the altar of Baal, and use the remnants of both to prepare a holy offering to the Lord God of Israel. Then he returns home for the night, unseen by any in the village. The village awakens to the destruction of their gods and idols, and they are angry. They begin a formal inquiry and discover Gideon to be the one who violated their communal worship.

Thankfully Gideon's father refuses to allow his neighbors to execute his son and gives support to Gideon's faithfulness. He pointed out that Baal should stick up for himself, if he's a real god. Thus, with a midnight raid and support from Dad, began the less-than-valorous career of Gideon, known also by the name Jeru-Baal, or "let Baal contend," a constant reminder of Baal's inability to fight back.

The political and military work of Gideon began in his own hometown and with Gideon as the enemy of his own people. Through much of the story, Gideon was not viewed as a hero. Gideon was maligned and hated even by his own community for reminding them of their *covenant* and calling them to obedience to their law and God.

In order to do the right thing, Gideon first had to sacrifice his own name and reputation to show that he was good and Godly. He had to learn how to be courageous. He had to learn how to be faithful. He had to brave the slings and arrows of his own people, his own tribe, in order to prepare himself to defend them against their foreign aggressors.

This is our journey today. It starts at home. One nation, under God. Indivisible with liberty and justice for all.

As a veteran, I read the story of Gideon and I reflect on the values that Gideon shares with a warrior. The story of Gideon reminds us that we are not only fighting a battle against foreign enemies. Sometimes the fight must begin with a struggle against domestic enemies. Those who would violate the Covenant that binds us as a community of faith and that grants us blessing.

This is what our warriors face in today's military. In the old days of endless wars, we spoke of mission creep, the slow and unplanned shift of objectives resulting in a quagmire. In today's military we can rightly speak of the loss of our fundamental purpose, our common creed—our covenant. The "mission creep" is inside our ranks, as our original purpose as warriors and servants of the Constitution has transformed into an austere bureaucracy hell-bent on ideological conformity and societal change.

There's one more lesson we can learn from Gideon, though. Throughout this book, I've praised the virtue of "readiness." But the story of Gideon is a good reminder that readiness means nothing without God. God chose "unready" men to accomplish his purposes. We're not supposed to admire Gideon's cowardliness or hesitance—the Bible has far more admirable language for leaders like Joshua, who encourage us to "be strong and courageous"—but to remember that strength is nothing without righteousness. Just as America's military might is nothing without an unwavering commitment to the Constitution and the defeat of our enemies, internal and external.

In the end, Gideon also ends up getting lost in personal vengeance and fancying himself a king, naming his son Abimelech, or "my father is king." Any one of us could forget the covenant as Gideon did. But there's also grace for imperfect Gideon, who's named one of the heroes of the faith in the New Testament.

The fundamental purpose of every elected officer, official judge, law enforcer, or warrior is to protect and defend the Constitution of the United States against all enemies foreign and domestic. The inability of legions to recognize that this is the primary problem we face in the military is staggering. Remember, this book is not about "how the military went woke." It is about "how the military allowed itself to go woke." When we lose sight of the fact that the primary responsibility of the president of the United States is to protect and defend the Constitution of the United States, then everything else falls apart. The military, our schools, and our entire social contract are based on this bedrock—and it's gone.

Our covenant is broken. Our next president has one last chance to repair it.

Chapter 14

MARXIST-ADJACENT MILITARY ACADEMIES

Properly understood, United States military academies have always been *military* educational institutions. Senior and retired officers considered it an honor to do a tour, or two, at West Point, Annapolis, or Colorado Springs to impart military knowledge on the next generation. It was also an opportunity for officers, and their families, to settle into a more predictable operational tempo for a few years—teaching classes on their subject matter expertise, at the pace of a university.

Over the years, and for various reasons, this changed. Civilian professors were welcomed on campus—for reasons of "diversity" as well as expediency. And with them came the predictable, radical, left-wing educational philosophies. I remember the nonsense some radical professors were spewing at Princeton University just days after 9/11, but thought it was confined to so-called "elite" civilian universities. Not the case. A former West Point professor recently told me, "Within two weeks of 9/11, some civilian professors were starting with the 'we deserved this' narrative. Talking about how this was payback for the crusades." Stunning.

Today, it's much worse. Most of the staff at all of the military academies are civilian professors. And, yes, most of them have the same political leanings as academia writ large. The combination of left-wing civilian professors, and woke guidance from Washington, DC, has transformed these institutions. Congressman Mike Waltz, himself a colonel, has a simple solution. A congressional panel he chaired wrote, "Congress should direct the service academies, to the maximum extent possible, to rely on uniformed military professors and Title 10 employees except when it is not possible to train a military member to perform those duties." All it would take is a new commander in chief who sees the danger to reverse it. But that's just a start, and we're not there yet. The Biden administration, instead, is the worst of all worlds.

One recent West Point graduate told me he experienced the shift in real time. Toward the end of his time at West Point, which corresponded with Joe Biden entering office, he endured lecture hall after lecture hall, mandatory brief after mandatory brief, about "white rage," "transgenderism," diversity/CRT training (one where *only* black cadets were allowed to talk), and even outright hostility to Donald Trump, while he was president—the commander in chief. *All* those ideas were also included in class, and all of this was pushed dutifully by both civilian professors and Pentagon leaders. Even the superintendent's office, I was told, was always tuned to CNN or MSNBC; FOX News was *not* allowed. It wasn't even hidden that West Point commandant General Darryl Williams was a hard-core Democrat. But it's not just West Point.

The United States Air Force has a mission-readiness requirement, like every other branch of the armed forces. On any given day they are required to have 80 percent of their airpower fully mission capable and ready to fly. Instead, the United States Air Force is more focused on Diversity, Equity, and Inclusion; and the Air Force's academy has civilian professors—like Lynn Chandler Garcia—writing op-eds in the *Washington Post* bragging about teaching Critical Race Theory. But surely, the Air Force still knows how to have their airplanes ready for combat? Not so. The new chairman of the Joint Chiefs of Staff, the former Air Force chief of staff "CQ" Charles Brown, could maintain only seven out of ten planes as combat ready, but found plenty of time to push a DEI/CRT agenda in his branch. CQ happens to be black, which doesn't matter to me one way or another, but means a lot to him. More on that in a moment.

The mighty F-35 was designed to take out Chinese and Russian aircraft before they left the runway. In 2023, the Air Force got a $15 billion upgrade on the F-35 and now leaders are recommending the fifth-generation fighter receive a sixth-generation replacement. But planes need pilots and maintenance, and General Brown had those fighters at 68 percent readiness for war in 2022. The F-22, the Air Force's stealth fighter of the future, stood at 50 percent readiness under General Brown. With CQ Brown, the Air Force got to celebrate its "first" minority chief of staff, yet it had planes that were not mission capable of defending American-controlled skies. So instead of making soldiers get better at flying airplanes, Secretary of Defense Austin changed the standard for what is considered "capable." General Brown quickly claimed it was a more "holistic view of readiness." Holistic, in case you didn't know, is Latin for *bullshit*.

Can't meet the standards? Just lower them.

Let's stick with ol' CQ for a moment, since he is the new chairman of the Joint Chiefs of Staff. Back in 2022, when CQ Charles Brown was in charge of the United States Air Force, he sent out an Air Force–wide memo to both the headquarters of the Air Force *Academy* and the Air Education and Training Command titled "Officer Source of Commission Applicant Pool Goals." He instructed all institutions to "develop a diversity and inclusion outreach plan" aimed at achieving specific racial quotas broken down by percentage for each race. He wanted "White" officer candidates at 67.5 percent and "Black/African American" officer candidates at 13 percent.

Governor George Wallace would be proud. Imagine, at a time when recruiting across all branches is missing their goals, General CQ believes now is the time to make *skin color* the primary factor for who should be admitted to the Air Force Academy, who should become an officer, and who should be promoted.

Sounds pretty racist to me. Textbook definition. Oh, and it's illegal. While so many woke liberals pride themselves on new DEI standards, they are (willfully) ignorant that color-blindness—meaning real equality—is already protected by federal statute. If a black American applies for any job, is qualified, and you reject them based on their skin color—that is illegal. You are breaking the federal law that has been on the books for decades. The United States Equal Opportunity Commission is clear when it states that no company or organization may "discriminate against a job applicant because of his or her race, color, religion, sex (including gender identity, sexual orientation, and pregnancy), national origin, age (40 or older), disability or genetic information." That's really broad, and the law of the land—but that's not good enough for CQ.

Title VII of the 1964 Civil Rights Act be damned, the chief of staff of the United States Air Force has his own race-based story and takes his personal emotional baggage and projects it onto everyone he meets. But CQ himself should know how far the Army has come: his father served two tours in Vietnam in the Army, retiring as a colonel, and his grandfather served in the Pacific in World War II. Even though times have changed—and this son of combat veterans has risen to the top of the American military—it's not enough. CQ Brown doesn't so much care if quality individuals serve at the Air Force Academy, so long as they all look different—or more like him. To supports his claims, CQ Brown loves to tell a (completely unsubstantiated) story about being in civilian clothes back when he was in charge of the Pacific Air Force Command.

As he once told the great military journalists at *People* magazine,

When you get to senior levels, you have reserved parking spots around the base. I was in civilian clothes, I parked in my spot and someone came out and said, "That slot is reserved for the Pacific Air Force's Commander." And I go, "Yeah, I know, because I am the Pacific Air Force's Commander." There was just an assumption there. Those stories stick with me, and it does bother me when people make assumptions before they have a chance to even know or meet me, or they assume I'm not qualified.

Assumptions, you say? Maybe an airman assumed the commander of the Pacific Air Force wouldn't be wearing Guess jeans and an Affliction T-shirt? Or maybe he drives a beat-up car? Or maybe the story is completely made up? We can't know. But here's something we do know: *your race, and his race, mean a lot to* CQ Brown. And the tragedy of these types of emotionally stunted, angry, race-based people is that they have an ax to grind—and will grind it. Take it to the racist bank: black troops, at all levels, will be promoted simply based on their race. Some will be qualified; others will not be. With the Pentagon now run by, and fully staffed by, so-called "leaders" like CQ Brown, we can assume that 17 percent of all black officers in the Air Force are promoted simply because of how they look—and not because of how they lead.

And that is a sin, a damned sin. It means, in some cases, incompetent leaders will be picked or promoted because of their skin color. And if those leaders suck, their troops will suffer. And, since the military is in the kill-or-be-killed business, they will get people killed. In other cases, competent military leaders will be picked or promoted because of their merit. And even if those leaders are fantastic, the perception of their troops will be that they didn't earn that slot—creating a toxic environment. Once again, the kill-or-be-killed business is undercut at the altar of racial benchmarks our country made illegal sixty years ago.

As of the writing of this book, CQ Brown replaced Mark Milley as the chairman of the Joint Chiefs. Back to the previous paragraph—was it because of his skin color? Or his skill? We'll never know, but always doubt—which on its face seems unfair to CQ. But since he has made the race card one of his biggest calling cards, it doesn't much matter. And since we know Joe Biden isn't really running the country—it's safe to assume that CQ Brown is running the world. DEI has gone global—long live the free world!

Each military branch has a four-star general as its chief of staff. And one four-star general is the "chief" of all the joint branches combined. The chairman of the Joint Chiefs is America's highest-ranked officer— and the chief advisor to the president of the United States.

The military standards, once the hallmark for competency, professionalism, and "mission first" outcomes, have officially been subsumed by woke priorities. You think CQ Brown will think intuitively about external threats and internal readiness? No chance. He built his generalship dutifully pursuing the radical positions of left-wing politicians, who in turn rewarded him with promotions.

Advance DEI/CRT in the ranks ... promote him!

Convert the naval fleet to a futile "green" future ... promote him!

Focus on "extremism" in the ranks without evidence except some story about a parking spot ... promote him!

We are led by fools, starting at the top.

So where does this viewpoint come from? Celebrating "firsts," while lowering standards? If you are going to radically change the military for the long haul, you have to start with new officers. They must have a new standard. And the academies that create those officers are the clearinghouse.

At West Point, the US Army's esteemed military academy, the DEI plan for 2020 to 2025 was front and center for all cadets. LTG Darryl Williams, then the superintendent at West Point, released a five-year plan that focused on "inclusivity" as *equal in importance* as marksmanship under fire. To be sure, the enemy doesn't believe that to be the case. According to LTG Williams, "competing with the civilian sector for the highest quality recruits" was predicated on Critical Race Theory (CRT) and Diversity, Equity, and Inclusion (DEI). It is gospel at West Point, and it is everywhere.

This was met with outrage by a legendary list of generals and alumni of West Point yesteryear. They wrote an open letter titled "Declaration of Betrayal of West Point and the Long Gray Line," in May 2022, signed by "Concerned Graduates of West Point." Notable signatories included military legends LTG Thomas McInerney, USAF (Ret) Class of 1959; MG Paul E. Vallely, US Army (Ret) Class of 1961; and Colonel Andrew O'Meara, US Army (Ret). In that letter, they dropped neutron bombs of truth, explaining how this is way beyond bad policy—it's a fundamental attack on our shared values, culture, and virtues as a society:

> *Leftist ideologues are trying to replace personal responsibility, self-reliance, and initiative with the entitlement mentality. They are working hard to transform the Constitution into a document that can be continually revised to accommodate the latest socio-cultural trends. By mandating the instruction of Critical Race Theory to every citizen serving in the military, they establish Critical Race*

*Theory as the fundamental principles upon which Socialists de-
mand soldiers, sailors, airmen, marines, midshipmen, and cadets
serve. The military indoctrination in Critical Race Theory is considered necessary to prevent internal opposition to an attempted
coup from within the ranks of the military (white extremism).*

    *Critical Race Theory brands the founders as evil, the Consti-
tution as illegitimate, and the Republic as systemically racist. It
abolishes the Declaration of Independence that declares all men
are created equal. It brands the population as racist, privileged, and
unfit to enjoy the rights of citizenship. It is a call to overthrow the
government we served to preserve freedom and government by, for
and of the people. This is no time for summer soldiers and sunshine
patriots. Those who have stood in harm's way are needed now to
stand by our oath. It is time to speak truth to power. We either serve
Duty, Honor, Country, or we challenge the demands of a secular
revolution to fundamentally alter America transforming the Republic into a socialist police state.*

Amen, gentlemen.

West Point wasn't the only military academy facing a new DoD in-
terpretation of what domestic enemies looked like. The United States Air
Force Academy in Colorado Springs was right there with West Point.
An op-ed published in the *Washington Examiner* in June 2023 was written by an Airman at the Air Force Academy so afraid of retaliation from
his superior officers that he used the pseudonym "Evan Smith."

He explained that "during a DEI briefing," airmen got a lecture on
how they should not "refer to our parents as 'mom and dad' because it was
'divisive language because everyone might not have a mom and a dad.'"

What else could be going on? To his regret, he can't say, because
"after media exposure"—that is to say, FOX News' reporting—"all DEI

training is being presented as controlled unclassified information" and airmen were warned that if they revealed "these trainings to outside sources, we could face prison time."

So, it's not about the training. It's about *not* allowing the American media, meaning the American public, to see that training. Not only are we telling our future combat officers that they can't refer to their parents as "mom and dad," but we are also attempting to make this DEI training controlled and secret so that the American people cannot discover what our tax dollars are producing. "Evan Smith" went on to explain that:

> *The majority of cadets do not like this training and see it as divisive and bad for morale. But the academy continues to elevate the voices of cadets who agree with the training and want to spread leftist ideology further.*

Naturally, bad ideas love an echo chamber. Never mind the fact that most cadets live in the real world; let's cater to the exceptions. Smith's conclusion paints a grim picture of how many sensible young people now have to suppress their common sense to rise through the ranks.

> *Though I may not agree with the teachings of the Air Force Academy's DEI program, I will continue to sit through the divisive briefings and boring lectures because one day, I will be on the other side, and I will teach my airmen about how we are united by what brings us together: our national identity as Americans.*
>
> *Regardless of race, sex, or ethnic backgrounds, we are all Americans, and we are all united under the values outlined in the Declaration of Independence and the Constitution. The ideals*

in those documents, not an ideology that teaches us to look at each other through the lens of race and division, are what have and will continue to guide our military and our nation through future conflicts.

United, we stand. Divided, we fall.

"Evan Smith" is exactly the type of young Airman that will lead his peers' children in the worst of times on behalf of America. *If he makes it.* And when he doesn't, this was what our military will be missing. His mindset, his determination to do what is right, gives me some hope that America's future generations will die safe and free. "Smith" was what Sojourner Truth was referring to when she said, "Truth is powerful, and it prevails." Question is: Are there enough "Evan Smiths" out there anymore?

So how did this all happen at our military academies? Is it enough to just pile this atop the dumpster fire of the Biden administration? Well, in fact . . . yes.

In 1972, the Federal Advisory Committee Act created a Board of Visitors (BOV) for the military academies. They are tasked with oversight of each of the military academies. They are charged with reporting to the president and the secretary of defense, as well as the Armed Service Committees of both the House and the Senate, things like morale, discipline, curriculum, instruction, and academic methods. Each branch academy has six members appointed by the president of the United States, for three-year terms. The vice president nominates three members; the Speaker of the House nominates four members, all for a one-year term. The Senate and House Armed Services Committee each get one member to appoint for one year.

When a new president is elected, it is customary that, unless there is a controversy or issues with character, the BOV stays through their entire term and the incoming commander in chief or House Speaker, etc., nominates their own members to the BOV. This was the tradition of the United States Military Academies until . . . President Joe Biden. On January 30, 2021—just ten days after being sworn in—Biden had his new secretary of defense suspend the Board of Visitors. Then, in a drastic purge, all eighteen Donald Trump–appointed BOV members were told to resign or be fired by close of business on September 8, 2021. A week later, Secretary of Defense Lloyd Austin created subcommittees, not approved by the charter in 1972 by Congress, and even gave authority to nonmembers of the BOV for the Army, the Navy, and Air Force academies.

So if you are planning a coup d'état to overnight transform military academy curriculum into DEI and CRT, you employ unprecedented and illiberal tactics to assure "gender equity" and "racial theory." You remove the other party and install your own, tradition be damned. There was outrage (really only at FOX News) about this purge, but the administration was undeterred. Radical transformation was far more important.

Academy cadets now learn that "positive white identity is an impossible goal" and white people are "inherently racist," according to Air Force civilian professors and West Point instructors. The same is happening at all of the core military academies in America.

* * *

Enter the Supreme Court, kind of. In June of 2023, "Students for Fair Admissions" won a stunning Supreme Court victory against Harvard University and the University of North Carolina, essentially ending race-based admissions in universities across America. The court ruled that their consideration of race in college admissions violates the Fourteenth

Amendment's equal protection clause. Of course higher ed is already working to circumvent it, but the ruling is clear: the Supreme Court has just overturned affirmative action in the *SFFA v. Harvard* decision. The court ruled that race cannot be used as an advantage in college administration.

But there was an asterisk. At first, the high court exempted military academies from their ruling. They didn't explicitly say military academies *can* consider race; they just declined to rule on their status—deferring to the executive branch's oversight of national security and the military. It was disappointing to see the conservative court punt on this question.

But then the other shoe dropped. Students for Fair Admissions brought an emergency request in 2024 that would have forced West Point to pause the practice of race-based admissions, until another case involving two cadets made its way through lower courts. Instead, in February 2024, the Supreme Court declined a request to block West Point from using race as a factor in admission decisions. The Biden administration argued vigorously to keep race-based admissions, arguing "a diverse Army officer corps is a national-security imperative."

A future Trump administration would argue differently—which would breathe life into ending institutionalized racism in military academy admissions. The military is supposed to be the bedrock definition of a meritocracy. Every aspect of the armed forces is, or at least used to be, based on testing, qualification, physical training, and experience. There is no separate but equal in the military. There is one standard that men and women must comply with: the military standard. Today that means something very warped under the Biden administration; a new administration *must* change this.

But we're far from it. West Point recently adopted a new undergraduate field of study for cadets. Imagine this: the military academy responsible for some of the greatest warrior generals in the modern era now boasts a . . . Diversity & Inclusion Studies Minor (DISM). You know China is up at night worrying about this coming at them.

According to West Point,

Diversity and Inclusion Studies (DISM) is an interdisciplinary minor administered by the Department of Behavioral Sciences & Leadership that consists of humanities and social science courses. America is a multicultural polity and demands knowledgeable and pragmatic thinkers who understand the range of human experiences. The DISM helps fulfill the Superintendent's and Dean's vision for diversity and inclusion at West Point. Moreover, the DISM at West Point offers cadets a framework for critically and creatively thinking about the broader impact of diversity and inclusion at the individual, organizational, societal, and/or global levels.

This five-course minor includes classes like PL377: Social Inequality, N352: Power and Difference, SS392: The Politics of Race, Gender, and Sexuality. However, you must take one of four classes to qualify, they include: HI391: World Religions (especially Islam, of course), HI461: Sex and Civilizations (you knew it), HI463: Race, Ethnicity, Nation (in no specific order), and HI398: Society & Culture in American History (according to the hosts of *The View*). I guess we can expect guest lecturers like Robin DeAngelo from *White Fragility* and maybe someone from the Broadway cast of *Hamilton*.

Karl Marx would be proud (Dwight Eisenhower, not so much). They say that red goes with everything, including digital camouflage. Our future military officers are now on the same ideological path as Che Guevara. The American people have no idea what their Department of

Defense has been doing since Biden was elected. Democrats in Congress support these changes, and Republicans are powerless (and toothless) in reversing these unconstitutional practices. It's straightforward: The Constitution is our lodestar. Marxists hate the Constitution. DEI and CRT are Marxist philosophies. Therefore DEI and CRT are enemies of our Constitution—domestic enemies.

The fight for freedom can only be won when there is meritocracy in our military—starting with a new courageous commander in chief. Maybe then our military academies will get back to creating color-blind *warriors*, not ethnic and gender studies cultists.

Epilogue

A LETTER TO MY SONS

Dear Boys,

God granted me the greatest possible gift—being your father. It is the highest honor I can imagine, and I take nothing more seriously—and nothing brings me greater earthly joy. I teach you, train you, discipline you, and challenge you—because I love you. I love you, like only a father can.

You are all individuals, with different gifts, interests, and passions. Each a child of God—and soon, I pray, men of God. You grew up in a covenant Christian home, which is the most important part of who you—and we—are. Our eternal home is in Christ's Kingdom, and we strive to love Him with all our heart, and soul, and mind. While we have breath, we are also charged with advancing His Kingdom here on earth.

To that end, you are blessed to have been born in the greatest country in human history. You have all studied history, extensively. There have been kingdoms, empires, tyrants, and tribes over thousands of years—but none like America. Our Founding Fathers understood that this experiment in self-governance and individual freedom was just that . . . an experiment. It was the exception to human history, not the rule. It had never been tried.

Almost 250 years later, our Republic still stands. America is still here, but she is on life support. We have turned our back on God, and on our founding principles. We have lost our way.

But we only got this far because men and women—but mostly men—were willing to fight for that freedom, with their "lives, their fortunes, and their sacred honor." Many of those men wore a uniform and carried a rifle—from the bridges of Lexington and Concord to the battlefields of Baghdad and Kabul. America is special because it is free, but only free because of special men.

Fighting men.

If you've read this book, you know a portion of your father's journey—from fighting extremists to being deemed one himself. It's a cautionary tale, for sure. But would I change one thing? Absolutely not. Next to serving God, wearing the uniform of the United States of America is the greatest thing I've ever done. Forget basketball. Forget the Ivy League. Forget television. Leading men in combat, with a shared mission—for my country—was the best education I ever received.

Yet we are at a crossroads. The military I joined in 2001 is not the military of today. It has been captured by leftist forces that have captured the rest of our culture. But unlike schools, unlike churches, and unlike different states, we can't just replace one we don't like with one we like better. We have one Pentagon. One military. One Army. If we lose those, we have truly lost America.

It is up to my generation—in government, media, and culture—to fight for a change in leadership inside our military. It is an uphill battle to right that ship. But it is up to your generation, even in the face of serious headwinds, to fill the ranks from the inside and impact it from within. It's up to you to decide if service to country is still worth it.

Is America still worth fighting for?

Is America still worth dying for?

By the time you each reach eighteen years of age, we will know more about the answer to those questions. And I will be there to counsel you.

Even with those questions—and even with all the uncertainty—I hope you join the ranks of American fighting men. I encourage you to serve, asking yourself this simple question: *If not me, then who?* If not Gunner, Jackson, Boone, Luke, or Rex Hegseth—who is going to protect America? Are you going to rely on other men, or on women, who have other worldviews to fill the ranks? Just because our military is far from perfect, can we afford to lose her? My answer is no.

If you take that oath, I hope you take it all the way. Your dad didn't know the difference between the Army and the Marine Corps when he joined. I was not from a military family. But when you join, you will know. And I would urge you to join *the best*. The SEALs. The Rangers. The Green Berets. Marine Raiders. Not only will you learn the most about yourself, get the best training, and do the most good for your country, but those units are also the *least likely*—still today—to be infected by the woke virus. Elite units usually skip most of—excuse my language but it's true—the *bullshit*.

If my boys are going to raise their right hand, and put the American flag on their shoulders, I want them where it matters. Where real decisions are made, and where meritocracy—for the most part—still reigns. Service to country, with God in your hearts, will take you places and teach you things you will *never* learn anywhere else. You will be forged, you will be warriors, and you will never regret it. You will join another brotherhood, an elite brotherhood.

I urge you in this consideration to show courage. You are men. *Act like it*. But if you choose not to serve in uniform, that is your choice. Then my charge for you is to fight and lead at home—because our war is on all fronts.

I love you boys—and pray that your fight, like mine, means your kids (and may you have many!) and my grandkids live in an America that honors God, cherishes freedom, celebrates families, and lives in peace.

In God We Trust,

Dad

Acknowledgments

First and foremost, all glory to Jesus Christ—our Lord and Savior. Without him, I would not be here today. (And *please* forgive the foul language in this book; you can take the man out of the Army, but I'm still working on getting the Army out of the man.)

Always—love, thanks, and appreciation to my incredible wife, Jenny. Thank you for supporting me in this project every single day. You, my dear, are also a warrior.

Deepest thanks to my dear friend and Army badass David Bellavia. Your input, writing, editing, and feedback were indispensable to this project. This book does not happen without you.

Finally, thank you to FOX News, *FOX & Friends*, FOX Nation, FOX Books, and HarperCollins for believing in, and supporting, this project.

About the Author

PETE HEGSETH is the cohost of *FOX & Friends Weekend*, America's number one–rated cable morning television show. He also hosts multiple programs on FOX Nation.

Pete is an Army veteran of Afghanistan, Iraq, and Guantanamo Bay who holds two Bronze Stars and a Combat Infantryman's Badge for his time overseas.

Pete is the author of several books, including *Battle for the American Mind*, which spent more than twelve weeks on the *New York Times* bestseller list, including four straight weeks at number one.

Pete has a bachelor's degree from Princeton University and (used to have) a master's degree from Harvard University—but he mailed it back, because Harvard is a leftist indoctrination camp.

Pete and his wife, Jenny, live in middle Tennessee and have seven children—all of whom they pray grow up to be warriors for God and country.